M. (Jacques-Vincent) Delacroix

The Memoirs of an American

Vol. 2

M. (Jacques-Vincent) Delacroix

The Memoirs of an American
Vol. 2

ISBN/EAN: 9783744715744

Printed in Europe, USA, Canada, Australia, Japan

Cover: Foto ©Suzi / pixelio.de

More available books at **www.hansebooks.com**

THE

MEMOIRS

OF AN

AMERICAN.

VOL. II.

THE

MEMOIRS

OF AN

AMERICAN.

WITH A

DESCRIPTION

OF THE

KINGDOM of PRUSSIA,

AND THE

ISLAND of St. DOMINGO.

Tranſlated from the FRENCH.

IN TWO VOLUMES.

VOL. II.

LONDON:

Printed for F. and J. NOBLE, at their reſpective
Circulating Libraries, near *Middle Row*, *Holborn*,
and *Saint Martin's Court*, near *Leiceſter Square*.

M DCC LXXIII.

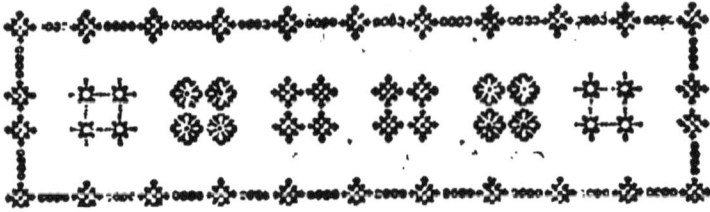

MEMOIRS

OF AN

AMERICAN.

It had now been more than a month upon the wide ocean which feparates Europe from America, when a favourable trade wind carried us towards the ifland which gave

B me

me birth.   One day that Mr. Marſilla,
the mate of the ſhip, and myſelf, were
walking on the deck, we admired the
pure and unclouded ſky, and its reſplen-
dent azure roof, the ſinking ſun yet
darted its rays in the air, but the wide
ocean ſeemed to open a boſom to receive that brilliant orb, as the evening
now approached. We perceived, all of
a ſudden, a freſh cold breeze which
curled the waves, the heavens ſoon became overcaſt, and the waves ſwelled,
and were ſhortly covered with foam.   I
foretold to Mr. Marſilla a violent tem-
peſt, and deſired him to deſcend.   The
young mate prevented him, and laugh-
ed at my fear.   The night advanced,
and we could ſcarce diſtinguiſh objects

the

the nearest to us. As I was going off the deck, a large sea broke upon our quarter; happily for me I had fast hold of the ropes, but heard a violent scream immediately. I called several times to Mr. Marsilla and the mate, but received no answer, and I immediately suspected they had both of them been washed overboard. The sailors, frighted by my suspicion, immediately backed the sails. I presently afterwards met the captain, to whom I communicated my fears. He ordered Mr. Marsilla and the mate to be sought for, but we were soon confirmed in the truth of my suspicions. Mrs. Marsilla, from whom it was impossible to conceal the melancholy catastrophe, was in the greatest

agonies;

agonies; fhe attempted to throw herfelf into the fea, it was fcarce poffible
to prevent the effects of her defpair.
The danger had caft a fear throughout
the fhip, our veffel was as nothing before the winds, fhe mounted with the
roaring waves, and feemed prefently afterwards to fink into the deep abyfs.
The night was exceedingly dark, except
at intervals, when the forked lightning
glanced [1] upon the waves. With my
eyes fixed upon the water, I fought,
with but little hope, a glimpfe of the
friend I had loft. The vivid lightning afforded a tranfient light upon
the waves around us, and I thought I
could once difcover fome perfon ftruggling againft the waves. His ftrength
                                      feemed

feemed increafed upon the fight of the veffel, towards which he extended his hands; but darknefs immediately fucceeded, and I could fee no more. I informed the failors of what I had obferved, who called with all their ftrength, at the fame time throwing out ropes; but the noife of the thunder and waves drowned their ufelefs clamours. Infpired with hope, I threw into the air a rope lighted at the end feveral times, and all the failors did the fame. By the light of one which I threw, I thought I could again perceive the unfortunate being. He feized it with his hands, I was prefently fenfible of the refiftance, and therefore called for more help. Wonderful efcape! I flipped down the

fide

fide of the veffel, and hawled the almoft expiring body into the fhip.   I
could fcarce know my dear friend Marfilla again, he was fo much disfigured.
Exhaufted with fatigue, he could not
fupport his head, and ftill grafped, vio-
lently, the cord which had faved him.
I am unable to defcribe the joy, the ecftafy of his wife, when fhe was informed, that her hufband, whofe death fhe
lamented, yet lived, and was aboard the
fhip. Whilft they got off Mr. Marfilla's wet clothes, his wife chafed him
with her warm hands. The furgeon,
after making him throw up the water
he had fwallowed, had him put into a
warm bed. Whilft he repofed, we confidered his good fortune as a miracle;

his

his wife took my hands and kiffed them with tranfport in the excefs of her gratitude: the unfortunate mate was never feen more.

The winds were fhortly difperfed, a calm fucceeded the tempeft, and the rays of the rifing fun again fhone upon the water. Contemplating on that vaft ocean, the fea, where the largeft veffel is only as a grain of fand in fize; infenfible as we are, I faid to myfelf, how will intereft thus lead us into the midft of dangers? Why fhould we change into evil, the good which the Author of nature has deigned to create for the prefervation of his work? If the impetuous winds fwell the waves, and raife a

tempeft,

tempeft, is it not to purify that ele-
ment, that the continued calm, by cor-
rupting the ftagnant air, fhould not deftroy thofe who breathe it ? Oh men,
who fear death, do not feek it ; do not
go beyond the bounds nature has pre-
fcribed; do not confide in a perfidious
calm ; to-morrow the fmooth furface
may be ruffled by the wind ; the waves,
white with foam, will prefent to your
terrified minds deep pits, where death is
inevitable, and then you will lament
your departure from the fhore.

After repofing myfelf for fome hours,
I returned to Mr. Marfilla, who was
now pretty well recovered from the
trouble which his fatigue and fear had

caft

caft him into. He had taken fome re-
ftoratives, which had recovered his fpirits, and brought his weak fibres to their
wonted ftrength ; but his voice was
ftill feeble. Whilft I had been abfent,
his wife had informed him that he owed
his life to me ; therefore, as foon as I
entered, he took my hand and carried
it to his lips, at the fame time his tears
ftole down his cheeks. Affected with
his gratitude, I could not prevent my
tears mingling with his.

In a few days Mr. Marfilla was per-
fectly recovered. I was exceedingly happy in the thoughts of my having fnatched him out of the arms of death, and
reftored life to that virtuous, tender wo-

man,

man, who could not have furvived his lofs.

We now approached the ifland of St. Domingo, where my family lived in fplendor. An unhappy uncertainty ftill affected me; I fcarce dared to flatter myfelf with feeing my mother again. I was afraid fhe would ftill preferve her refentment, which had caufed her indifference as to my fate; that pride would fupprefs the joy which every mother muft feel upon the fight of a fon after many years abfence. At the time thefe unhappy thoughts affected me, Mr. Marfilla came up to me, and faid in the language of friendfhip, " I " fee you do not think me worthy your " confi-

" confidence; I am fure you are not
" happy, but you conceal the caufe,
" and refufe the affections of a man
" whofe life you have faved. My dear
" friend," he continued, " can you
" doubt my zeal, my gratitude, or the
" real fatisfaction I fhould enjoy in
" contributing to your happinefs ?"

The expreffion which appeared in the
eyes of that excellent young man, and
the truth of what he faid, affected me
greatly.

" Yes, my dear Marfilla, I am un-
" happy," replied I, " and it increafes
" upon my nearer approach to that
" ifland, where happinefs, which has

B 6 " fhunned

" fhunned me fo long, ought to fuc-
" ceed. But, my friend," I continued, " how can I inform you of the
" caufe of my diftrefs ? — That fecret
" belongs to another." As I pronounced
thefe words, the two ladies, whom virtue and affection had ftrictly united,
came up to us.

" I am right in my fufpicions," faid
Mr. Marfilla to his wife: " the friend
" whom we love to excefs is not happy,
" diftrefs rends his generous foul: Alas,
" if he dares not confide his misfor-
" tunes in us, who fhall be his com-
" forter ?"

" What

" What my hufband confiders as a
" duty in himfelf not to reveal," replied
the woman I adored, " I will impart to
" you; as I am certain of preferving
" your efteem and affection after the re-
" cital."

Her friend embraced her with tendernefs, and Mrs. Marfilla took hold of
her hand, whilft with courage fhe informed them of the fecret of her birth :
fhe told them with inimitable grace the
misfortunes of her mother, unhappily
brought to the grave by the perfidy of
her lover : fhe fpoke with the greateft
affection and gratitude of the many good
offices of her benefactrefs, and the love
of her hufband : fhe informed them of
the

the cruel revolutions which had changed our happy days into unhappy ones, and compelled us to go into a diftant country, where we met only with humiliation and defpair; fhe likewife informed them, that my mother entertained fuch contempt for her, and was fo irritated at my marriage, that fhe had conftantly refufed, ever fince fhe had been informed of it, the fmalleft affiftance, and had anfwered my letters with the greateft difdain, commanding me never to write more. " Judge then," fhe continued, " if in our defign of prefenting our-" felves before her, we have any rea-" fon to expeft a more favourable re-" ception."

" No,

" No, my tender friend," replied Mrs.
Marfilla to her, " you fhall not be expof-
" ed to the contempt of that unjuft
" parent; you fhall go with us to our
" houfe; and if your hufband's mo-
" ther refufes to fee you, we will re-
" turn to France together accompanied
" by our hufbands; my father expects
" only two children, but he fhall be
" father to four. With what pleafure
" will he receive us," fhe continued,
looking at me; " how much will the
" tendernefs of his careffes be increaf-
" ed, when he is informed that you
" faved the life of his daughter's huf-
" band!"

Full

Full of gratitude, we chearfully ac-
cepted the offers of that generous woman.

Happy now as to the fate of my
wife, I enjoyed all the charms of friendſhip; I no longer imagined that I ſaw
my beſt-beloved inſulted, rejeƈted by
my family, and return to me diſſolved
in tears; I now no longer murmured
at the injuſtice of men. I thought with
pleaſure on ſeeing her one day cheriſh-
ed by thoſe who now depiſed her, be-
cauſe they had not yet ſeen that beautiful face, which was the emblem of her
mind. This happy thought made me
wiſh to conceal her arrival from my mother, and preſent myſelf alone before
                                    her,

her, and have my wife afterwards introduced to her under a fictitious name. Mr. and Mrs. Marfilla approved my scheme, and promifed their utmoft endeavours to infure its fuccefs.

We were now within view of my native land, from whence I had been carried into diftrefs and mifery. We perceived the flying enfign, which declared the arrival of our fhip to the colony. Whilft we were at fome diftance from the port, a fhallop came alongfide to reconnoitre us. Mr. Marfilla and his wife, my wife and myfelf, defcended into it, and went immediately afhore.

Wherefore,

Wherefore, when I have more misfortunes to defcribe, fhould I not lay afide my pen? What pleafure can I propofe to myfelf in the remembrance of my paft fufferings? — Alas! does not the lover who has loft the object of his affection, ftill look upon her portrait with innate pleafure? He loves to contemplate her features, and bathe them with his tears; he is fearful left his affection fhould become weaker; he is not willing that the wound in his heart fhould be healed; he prefers the lonefome and folitary places which feed his melancholy, to the gay meadows enamelled with flowers; the chearful gaiety of the rural nymph is difpleafing; the warbling of the birds on the trees

fatigue

fatigue his ear; his unfociable eye en-
joys the profundity of a precipice;
the mountains covered with fnow are
fuch as he loves to pafs over; he wifhes
that his plaintive notes might fill the
air.

A frightful recollection, the moft
melancholy ideas begin to environ me;
my imagination becomes clogged with
them, my hand trembles, and my heart
is in violent agitation. Infenfible creature! thus to feek unhappinefs, and even
death.

After fome days refidence in the
houfe of my friend Marfilla, I went to
that of a fifter, whom, at my departure

ture from St. Domingo, I had left very
young.   As I went acrofs the court before her houfe, I met an elderly lady
in a chair carried by negroes.   She
looked earneftly at me, as well as I at
her.   I went forward towards a faloon,
where I was introduced to my fifter's
hufband, who received me with a cold,
conftrained politenefs.   His wife, who
appeared foon after, made me more
welcome ; her careffes were of the ten-
dereft kind, which I warmly returned.
She informed me, that her mother had
juft left her.   I then imagined that the
perfon whom I had met, and whofe face
occafioned me fome little confufion, was
the perfon who had given me birth.
My fifter afked me if I wifhed to fee
                                    her,

her, and offered to accompany me. " I
" have fcarce been a moment in your
" houfe," I replied, " and you are al-
" ready defirous of fending me away."
She bluſhed, and embraced me, at the
fame time aſſuring me of her friendſhip and affection.   She foon afterwards
led me to an apartment which ſhe in-
treated me to confider as my own, and
gave me a flave to attend and wait on
me.   She called her two fons, who immediately came in the moſt chearful,
fprightly manner to kifs me.   I took
them in my arms.   " Amiable chil-
" dren," I faid to myfelf, " you are
" dear to her who brought you into
" the world, you do not fear her an-
                              " ger;

" ger; how much happier is your lot
" than mine !"

The next day I defired my fifter to
inform my mother of my arrival, and
to endeavour to diffipate her refentment
againft me which I had fo little merit-
ed. At the moment fhe was promifing
me her fervice, two negroes appeared,
opened the door of the faloon, and pronounced the arrival of my mother. My
fifter made me a fign to be filent, and
not difcover myfelf. When I faw
that venerable woman appear, already
funk in years, weak and enfeebled by .
long difeafes, I felt the fincereft love
and refpeft for her; I could fcarce contain my tranfports; I wifhed to throw
myfelf

myſelf at her feet, and preſs her hand
to my lips; I beheld her with reverence.
When I heard her call my ſiſter by the
tender name of daughter, I turned a-
way my head, to conceal my diſtreſs.
" Am I not alſo your ſon?" I ſaid to
myſelf. " Why ſhould you not acknow-
" ledge me ſuch?"

" I never had the honour of ſeeing
" that gentleman before," ſaid my mother, turning herſelf towards my ſiſter:
" does he belong to this part of the
" iſland?"

" He is a friend of my huſband's,"
replied my ſiſter, " juſt arrived from
" France."

" From

" From France !" faid my mother;
" Alas ! I had a fon there—"

" Has death deprived you of him ?"
interrupted I, in a feeble voice.

" He is alive for any thing I know,"
replied my mother; " but no longer fo
" to me."

She pronounced thefe laft words in a
manner which aftonifhed me; but looking at her daughter, " I am very good,
" I think," faid fhe to her, " thus to
" come to fee you every day."

" I am very grateful for the favour,
" my dear mother," replied my fifter.

Whilft

Whilft fhe finifhed thefe words, we heard a tumultuous kind of noife; the door opened, and the two children immediately ran to their grand-mother, who lavifhed her careffes on them: they prefently afterwards came to me, took me by the hand, and called me their dear uncle. My fifter immediately called them, and fent them away. My mother looked earneftly at me; fhe obferved my confufion and embarraff-ment, and began to fufpect who I was.

"What," faid fhe, "are you that "fon, who has difhonoured himfelf by "an unworthy alliance; who has taken "pleafure in precipitating himfelf into "indigence and infamy; who has at-

"tached

" tached his deftiny to that of an un-
" fortunate creature born in fin ?"

" Oh ! my mother," I cried, " what
" is it you are faying ?"

At that moment I faw her grow pale,
her eyes turned from me, and feemed to
avoid mine. My fifter flew to receive
her in her arms; I ran to her alfo, took
her hand and imprinted a thoufand
kiffes on it. She faw me at her feet,
and obferved my tears. Affected with
the fight, her tears ftole down her
cheeks, and for fome time fhe could
not utter her words.

" Unfortu-

" Unfortunate young man," fhe cried,
" 'you will be the death of me."

" Oh ! my dear, my tender mother,
" if you could but fee her who has ren-
" dered me criminal in your eyes—"

" I fee her ! I do not wifh," fhe continued, " to infult her in her diftrefs ;
" but I hope, at leaft, that you have fo
" much refpect for me as not to bring
" her into my prefence."

At thefe words I kiffed her hand, and
retired further : at that inftant my fifter's hufband made his appearance.

C 2   " Well,

" Well, Madam," faid he, "" you
" behold your fon, whom you thought
" you never more fhould have feen;
" will you not reftore him to your af-
" fection ?"

" If he was once dear to me," anfwered my mother, " ought he to have
" compelled me to hate him ?"

" Hate me!" I replied, " hate your
" child !—Oh ! my mother, that child
" always loved *you*."

She looked at me with more tendernefs;
my careffes, and my fifter's intreaties,
foftened her heart, and fhe called me
her fon. In the evening fhe permitted
me

me to conduct her to her houfe, which was at a little diftance from that of my brother-in-law, and fhe offered me an apartment to pafs the night in.

I was extremely impatient ——.return to Marfilla to fee my wife and friends again, to let them partake of my hope and joy, in my account of my interview with her whofe implacable hatred *I* feared; from which *they* formed the moft fanguine expectations.

" You will recover a mother," faid Mr. Marfilla to me, " and we, per- " haps, fhall lofe a friend."

" For

" For my part," replied his wife, looking tenderly at mine, " I am fure " of preferving this friend here :" and immediately thofe charming women, like two beautiful lilies which the gentle breeze only has feparated, embraced, and vowed eternal friendfhip to each other.

I had not even told my fifter that my wife was at St. Domingo: I was willing that fhe fhould be prefented by my friend as his relation; flattering myfelf that chance would one day make her known to my mother, from which event I hoped for every thing, as that tender woman feemed to attract the love of

all

all others, as by an irrefiftible charm.
My hope was not ill-grounded.

We had fcarce been a month at St.
Domingo, when Marfilla told my brother-in-law, with whom he had feveral
times before bartered for different things,
that he would one day bring Mrs. Marfilla, and prefent her to his wife; which
my brother feemed very defirous of.
The day they came to vifit my fifter,
I was there too, and pretended not to
know of their defign of coming. Some
days afterwards I accompanied my fifter to Mrs. Marfilla's, where my wife
faid a thoufand agreeable things, which
highly pleafed her. At our return, fhe
afked me what I thought of the niece

of Mr. Marfilla? meaning my wife. " She is well enough," I replied.

" 'Well enough!" fhe anfwered very tartly, " have you ever feen one more " amiable? As for myfelf, fhe appears " charming to me; and without being " willing to depreciate the merits and " accomplifhments of your Parifians, " I very much doubt whether you " could find one there to excel her."

I was pleafed with her admiration, and provoked her to go further, by fay-ing, " What is it, pray, that you find " fo aftonifhing in her?"

" She

" She has," fhe replied, " in the firft " place, a very noble, engaging coun- " tenance, which upon acquaintance " appears as the index of her mind; " a happy choice of expreffion, a fim- " plicity of manner at the time fhe is " faying a thoufand agreeable things, " which in other women would be ut- " tered with an air of importance; a " foft engaging manner at all times; " in fhort, fhe is in poffeffion of every " thing which enables our fex to tri- " umph over yours."

" Ah, but, fifter," I replied, " thofe " good qualities of hers, which feem to " aftonifh you fo much, all women are " in poffeffion of."

C 5

" That

" That is your French gallantry and
" politnefs, brother : for my own part,
" although a woman, I can with truth
" fay, that, among two thoufand whom
" I have feen, I know not one who re-
" fembles her. Thofe who have fenfe,
" depreciate or debafe in an unbecoming
" manner all thofe who furround them.
" If they are handfome, their manner
" always fays to all men, Adore me,
" but expect nothing in return; and
" deftroy, by their imperious and haugh-
" ty looks, all the effect of their charms.
" Others prefent a regular affemblage
" of features happily formed; but eve-
" ry one fays, after viewing them, Why
" has heaven refufed her fenfibility of
" foul? How much are thofe charm-
" ing

" ing faces expofed. by laughter with-
" out fenfe, by ftupid filence,. by an-
" fwers without precifion,, or, what is
" ftill worfe, by a proud. and haughty
" difpofition! I. do not. mention thofe·
" who poffefs neither. beauty nor good:
" qualities, but. there. are thofe who,
" poffefs neither."·

My. fifter's hufband. was of her opinion.; and they. together, after accufing.
me of injuftice,. compelled me to do·
homage to her. whofe fweetnefs and af-.
fability had fo much charmed them.. In:
the joy of. my. heart I faid to. myfelf,.
That beautiful creature will alfo fubdue·
her who now defpifes her, and. we fhall.
yet.be happy..

C. 6.   The:

The esteem of my sister for my wife,
made their mutual visits so frequent,
that they were almost always together.
My mother, when she saw her, to whom
a long series of misfortunes had given a
peculiar delicacy and softness, felt the
same affection for her which all did
who knew her. A most intimate friendship immediately succeeded. I had the
satisfaction of beholding her every day
surrounded by my family, which with
her great good qualities increased my
love every day. The kind of con-
straint which the presence of my relations imposed on me, contributed to
the pleasure which I experienced in
hearing and seeing her near me. The
dissimulation which made us reserved,
which

which fometimes prevented my careffes, my defires,, and the inchanting fmile which accompanied her refufal, all together increafed the fincere affection I had for her.

However, my mother always preferved an involuntary refentment againft the perfon whom fhe fuppofed my wife. The idea of my marriage never prefented itfelf, without her conceiving a violent diflike to me, and contempt for her who had deprived me of my liberty.

One day that we were alone, " My " fon," fhe faid, looking in an unhappy manner at me, " if you had, not " difpenfed with the firft law impofed
" by

" by nature on a child well bred; if
" you had refpected your mother and
" the honour of your family; if you
" had been cautious of imbittering the
" days of her who gave you life, by
" forming a fhameful difhonourable al-
" liance; foft pleafing hopes would play
" at this time round my heart: yes, I
" could then flatter myfelf with feeing
" you the hufband of a pretty, tender,
" and well-bred woman; at whofe ex-
" iftence we fhould have no reafon to
" blufh. I fhould have faid, with joy,
" when prefenting her to my friends,
" This is my daughter, this is the
" wife of my fon; I fhould not have
" trembled whilft informing them to
" whom fhe belonged; I fhould have
                            " openly

" openly named her parents ; then,
" tranquil and happy, I fhould have
" formed no wifhes but for the happi-
" nefs of my children; I fhould have
" congratulated myfelf on feeing them,
" and the worthy fruit of their love.
" Oh, my fon, why would you fo cru-
" elly affect me? By liftening to your
" defires, you have drawn misfortunes
" upon yourfelf, and difgrace to thofe
" belonging to you."

I could fcarce contain myfelf whilft
my mother was fpeaking; I wifhed to
difcover the perfon who appeared fo contemptible to her, to prefent her before
her, and fee her blufh at her injuftice
and cruelty. " But," fhe continued, in
a more

a more tender manner, " is the difeafe
" then without a cure? That woman
" to whom you have attached yourfelf,
" without having a proper power, for
" whom you have violated laws the moft
" facred, is fhe dearer to you than your
" mother? You cannot be ignorant,
" my fon, that the chain you formed
" unknown to me, at an age when your
", will ought to have been fubmitted to
" mine, juftice may break, and I de-
" mand of you to break it. Become
" free; you may affure the unhappy
" wretch an eafy fortune, and I promife
" you it fhall be better than fhe can
" have reafon to expect."

" What,

" What, my mother," faid I, inter-
rupting her, " do I hear this from you?
" Can this be a woman to whom ho-
" nour is fo precious, who thus advifes
" her fon to become perjured, to vio-
" late the moft folemn oath, to aban-
" don, to caft off, an unfortunate wo-
" wan, who has no other fupport than
" him? Alas! what has that tender
" virtuous woman done, that I fhould
" put her away? Would fhe receive
" prefents bafely offered by a criminal
" hand? I have not fold you my love
" and favours for money, fhe would
" fay; reftore me my innocence, and
" take your gifts away. No," I cried,
ftretching out my hands and clapping
them on my breaft, " No, good and
" virtuous

" virtuous woman, I will not add to
" thy misfortunes, by expofing you un-
" defervedly to the malicious cenfure
" of the world as an infamous crea-
" ture; the man you love will not thus
" wafte your tears; he already has fuf-
" ficient troubles, but the moft cruel
" would be to lofe the wife whom his
" heart has chofen."

" Oh, very well," replied my mother,
" preferve moft carefully that woman
" who is fo dear to you; prefer with
" her, fhame, indigence, I will not fay
" my hatred, as that can no way affect
" an unnatural child; pafs both of you
" your wretched days far diftant from
" a family, on whom you have firft
                              " brought.

" brought fhame by your unworthy
" love; never prefent yourfelf before
" me; you are no longer my fon; you
" have yourfelf renounced that title,
" by difpofing of your hand without
" my confent; you have trampled on
" all laws, you have defied me; but
" you fhall fuffer for it, your lot is
" caft."

She pronounced thefe laft words in a
terrible voice, her eyes became red with
paffion. I was fo affected, that I was
unable to anfwer her. I could only fay,
in a trembling voice, taking hold of her
hand, " Oh, my dear mother!" when
fhe pufhed me away, and immediately
quitted the room.

This

This converfation deftroyed all my hopes; with an almoft broken heart, I determined to diffipate my wretchednefs near my dearly beloved wife. and immediately retired thither. Some days had intervened fince my laft vifit there, becaufe my fifter had detained me to look over fome old papers, and fettle an affair which very much puzzled her hufband. When my arrival was pronounced, Mrs. Marfilla repeating my name, faid with a fmile to my wife, " Madam, do you know that gentle- " man?"

, " I believe I have feen him before," fhe replied, with a fmile, full of fweetnefs and love; " but it is fo long fince, " that

" that I have only a confufed idea of
" him."

The gaiety of thofe amiable women
infpired me with chearfulnefs.

" I fee," I replied, " that no perfon
" is fooner forgot than a hufband; I
" fhall therefore take care for the fu-
" ture not to abfent myfelf fo long."

" Sir," replied that charming woman
whom I adore, " have you the honour
" of being married, and dare abfent
" yourfelf fo long a time from your
" wife? There is great reafon to be-
" lieve that fhe is not your wife."

" Alas,

" Alas," I faid to myfelf, " they
" are willing to deprive me of that ti-
" tle. She is mine," I continued, raifing my voice, " fhe is the happinefs of
" my life," taking her in my arms at
the fame time. I was unwilling, left I
fhould efface her joy, to relate the converfation of the morning with my mother. I faw my dear Marfilla prefently appear; I put away my chagrin, and
gave myfelf up to the tranfports of love
and friendfhip.

The next day, that dear woman, who
fo well underftood how to read my very heart, and difcover all its motions,
feeing me uneafy and unhappy, imagined that fome new mortifications threaten-

ed

ed us.   She queftioned me ; I was willing to diffemble, but her fears were increafed.   I found myfelf forced to recite
to her the converfation which I had had
with my mother.   After my affuring
her that I had not difcovered the fecret
of our marriage, fhe refolved to go to
fee her; fhe flattered herfelf with re-
conciling two hearts which pride and
prejudice had feparated ; but prejudice
is oftentimes ftronger than reafon.

My wife was immediately conveyed
to my mother's houfe, when fhe found
her ftill reftlefs.   Whether her prefence
again brought to her remembrance the
difpute of the preceding day, or whether

ther her diftrefs became more violent,
I know not.

" Madam," faid my wife to her, " I
" am afraid I am come at a time that
" my company is troublefome."

My mother affured her of the pleafure fhe took in feeing her, and defired her not to leave her. However,
an air of melancholy and fadnefs was
diffufed over her countenance; it was
eafy to difcover, notwithftanding her at-
tempts to hide it, that fhe was unhappy. My wife, after fome reflection,
appeared fenfible of her diftrefs, and
defired to know the caufe.

" Madam,"

" Madam," replied my mother, " it
" is of fuch a nature that it cannot be
" mentioned without fhame. You fee
" a moft unhappy mother, who will to
" the day of her death reproach herfelf
" for having given life to a fon who
" has imbittered her days, and difho-
" noured all his family."

My wife replied, that the few times
fhe had feen him, he appeared to her to
poffefs an excellent mind; that fhe had
never heard him mention his mother
but with the greateft refpect and tender-
eft affection.

" The impoftor !" cried my mother.
" If he had loved me, if he had re-

" fpected me—but, can I inform you
" of what I wifh I was ignorant my-
" felf? The wretch has bereft me of
" all hopes of happinefs."

" I do not wifh," replied my wife,
" to fearch into what you would wifh
" to have concealed; but fince your
" fon has a good and compaffionate
" mother, who interefts herfelf in his
" fate, I cannot place him amongft the
" number of the unfortunate."

" Madam, I can do nothing for
" him; it no longer depends upon me
" to break the fhameful bonds he has
" entered into, to reftore him to that
" honour which he has defpifed. If
" he

" he would, he might yet recover his
" liberty, and efface the blot which he
" has brought on himſelf and family;
" but, blinded by a fooliſh paſſion, he
" ſlights the counſels of friendſhip and
" maternal affection; he attends only
" to his love, and reckons as nothing
" the happineſs of his mother."

" Do him more juſtice, Madam;
" whoever ſhe is that is the object of
" his affection, I am certain you will
" always be dear to him; ſhe who has
" gained his heart muſt be very deſpica-
" ble, if ſhe effaces the pureſt ſenti-
" ments."

" Alas,

" Alas, Madam, fhe is an unfortu-
" nate creature born in obfcurity, with-
" out fortune, without parents—Yes,
" Madam, without parents."

" Unfortunate indeed! fhe has moft
" reafon to complain!"

" Undoubtedly fhe has reafon to com-
" plain. But ought my fon to have
" married her? If he felt fome incli-
" nation for her, might he not have
" offered her affiftance, fnatched her
" from indigence? I fhould not have
" thought his compaffion a crime :
" but to choofe her for a wife, to in-
" troduce her into a good family, to
" expofe himfelf to want, and at length
" to

" to the refentment of his parent, whom
" he has offended and debafed; is not
" this, Madam, the height of folly?
" After having carried it to fuch a de-
" gree as to entertain contempt and dif-
" dain for the author of his exiftence,
" can he ftill flatter himfelf with pre-
" tenfions to my friendfhip, to my
" heart? If there is an obedience due
" from children to parents, ought I to
" acknowlege him for my fon?"

" I will not attempt to vindicate him;
" he ought not to have difpofed of his
" hand without your confent: but per-
" haps the woman he has chofen is not
" fo contemptible—"

D 3

" I do

" I do not know the unfortunate be-
" ing; I never faw her; it is too much
" for me to complain inceffantly of the
" wife of my fon, and not dare to pro-
" nounce the name of mother before
" her."

" You will be her mother; could
" fhe defire a better?"

" What is that you fay, Madam?
" Shall I adopt as my child the off-
" fpring of crime and debauchery? The
" very thought makes me fhudder."

: " Though the child of fin, fhe may
" perhaps be virtuous."

" I hope

" I hope fo, Madam ; but my fon
" is not the lefs culpable."

" If he lofes your affection for ever,
" he would be too feverely punifhed
" for his offence."

" That will be to him the leaft of
" his troubles. Alas, how happy would
" he have been ! Yes," purfued my
mother, looking at my wife, " if he
" had paid his court to a fenfible and
" beautiful woman, who unites the
" charms of the perfon with the beau-
" ties of the mind, I dare flatter myfelf
" that fhe would not have difdained
" his affection, and that her hand would
" have been his reward."

D 4

The

The amiable perfon to whom this language was addreffed, turned away her eyes and blufhed.

" Charming girl !" continued my mother, " why were not his eyes plac-
" ed upon *you* the day that he deliver-
" ed himfelf up to that fatal paffion
" which deprived him of his reafon ?
" If he had feen *yon*, he would have
" adored you, he would have been
" your hufband, and I fhould have
" been honoured in calling you daugh-
" ter."

" Madam," replied my wife, in a feeble manner, " your fon would not
" have been more happy, and my
" fortune

" fortune would ftill have been the
" fame."

" My dear friend, do you fay, that
" he would not have been more happy ?
" Could the infenfible creature have
" complained ? would he not be fenfi-
" ble of the value of honour and vir-
" tue ?"

" Virtue and honour are often con-
" cealed under fhame and poverty."

" Madam," replied my mother, " I
" do not comprehend you : would you
" compare yourfelf to that obfcure girl,
" who never knew the authors of her
" days ?"

D 5   " Alas!

" Alas! who owes her more pity
" than myfelf? whom as cruel a fate—
" But I am going perhaps to make my-
" felf an object of contempt in your
" eyes."

" What do you wifh to fay, Madam?
" are you not the niece of Mr. Mar-
" filla? is he not your uncle?"

" Madam, I am an unfortunate wo-
" man, my misfortunes took place at
" my birth. The illuftrious name of
" my mother has not been able to pre-
" ferve the daughter from fhame. Wan-
" dering over the earth, which fhe
" moiftens with her tears, fhe is every
" where fubject to diftrefs and humilia-
" tion;

" tion; all hearts become callous at
" her approach; fhe is debafed, treated
" with rudenefs, and even heaven it-
" felf feems willing to punifh for his.
" pity the generous man who has taken
" care of her, and has not difdained.
" either her heart or hand."

At thefe words my mother appeared
fpeechlefs for fome time, fhe looked upon my wife with aftonifhment: furprife;
regard, and indignation, fucceeded alternately; fhe feemed willing to ftifle the
fentiment which fhe felt in her heart.

" Are *you* the unhappy girl who has
" led my fon aftray?" fhe faid. But
raifing her voice with paffion, as if re-

D 6 proach-

proaching herſelf for the tendernefs ſhe had till that time felt for her; " It is " very impudent of you to prefent " yourſelf before me when you know " my averſion."

" You will fee her no more, Ma- " dam," interrupted my wife in a foft and melancholy voice; " ſhe has too " much reafon to complain, and does " not deferve your hatred: ſhe will no " more expofe herſelf to your anger " and new affronts; ſhe will be ſilent in " her diftrefs, and ſhed her tears in fo- " litude, till death puts an end to her " misfortunes."

She

She immediately aróse, defired Mr. Marfilla's fervants might be called, and ftepped into the carriage, without my mother fhewing the leaft regret at offending her.

It is impoffible to defcribe my emotion and diftrefs, when, upon hearing the noife of the carriage in the court, I flew to my beloved, I perceived a handkerchief in her hand, drying her tears, and endeavouring to wipe away the figns of them. Her eyes, yet red, gave me a melancholy look; her countenance, all pale and wan, had loft its bloom. She refted her hand upon my arm to defcend. Affected with her diftrefs, I had fcarce courage enough to

afk

afk the caufe; but her voice was too weak at that time, and fhe anfwered me only with a figh. We went acrofs the court in filence: as foon as we entered the porch, we faw Mrs. Marfilla advancing to meet us. My wife threw herfelf into her arms, and, whilft preffing her to her bofom, faid to her, " Oh; " my good friend, do not abandon me; " I am too unfortunate."

She had fcarce pronounced thefe words, than, weak and trembling, fhe feated herfelf in an arm-chair: a flood of tears rolled down her cheeks. I held one of her hands, whilft her friend embraced her, and endeavoured to dry her tears; her breathing was fhort and laborious,

borious, her diftrefs almoft fuffocated her. I afked her inceffantly what had happened to her. Her eyes feemed armed with anger, fhe feemed to fhun my careffes, and endeavoured to get further from me. " What," faid I to her, " do you wifh to fhun me? are " the tender anxieties of your hufband " troublefome and difagreeable to you? " You feem to avoid the tendernefs of " him who loves you, who knows no " diftreffes but yours. Am I the in-" nocent caufe of the tears which you " fhed at this time?"

" Yes, undoubtedly you are the " caufe," fhe replied; " but I do not " wifh to reproach you. You have been " defirous

" defirous of making me happy, and
" you have heaped misfortunes and
" difgrace upon me. If you had left
" me in obfcurity, I fhould. not at
" this time have been an object of
" hatred; no one would have had any
" right to reproach me for my exift-
" ence; but now I am complained of,
" I am debafed and infulted: but I
" fhall not long be fo."

" Infulted!" I exclaimed, " infulted!
" you, who do honour to your fex!
" Oh! name the wretch to me, the
" barbarian who could infult the moft
" virtuous, the moft refpectable of wo-
" men. Yes," I continued in a high-

er

er tone of voice, " tell me his name,
" and he fhall die by this hand."

" Go then, foolifh man," my wife
replied, not a little terrified at my ferocious appearance, " go then and
" pierce thy mother's bofom: or ra-
" ther plunge the poniard in my heart;
" deliver me from the load of life, it
" is horrid to me. Yes, death is the
" only bleffing I feek for from men."

Affected at thefe expreffions, I kneel-
ed at her feet, and faid, " My deareft
" love, how can you be fo cruel as to
" wifh to die? Is your hufband no
" longer dear to you? Does he not
" infpire you with a defire to live?
                                    " Are

" Are you willing to leave him, and
" plunge him into anguiſh and de-
" ſpair?"

Mrs. Marſilla, diſſolved in tears, con-
jured her, in the warmeſt terms, not to
give herſelf up to ſuch exceſſive grief:
She careſſed her with the greateſt affection, and tenderly reproached her.
Preſſed by love and friendſhip, ſhe
yielded to our intreaties, and informed
us what had ſo deeply affected her. She
was ſtill ſo affected with it, that ſhe
omitted not even the moſt minute cir-
cumſtance of what had paſſed between
her and my mother; ſhe told us that
ſhe had formed the moſt ſanguine hopes,
when ſhe diſcovered my mother's wiſhes
for

for my being united to her. She had
never feen, fhe told us, fo rapid a
change in affection, and fuch infenfi-
bility, when fhe faw the unhappy caufe
of all her troubles. " Was it necef-
" fary," fhe continued, " to crofs the
" wide ocean, to expofe myfelf to all
" the dangers of a long voyage, to
" come into a ftrange world to feek
" humiliation and contempt, to be
" flighted by an unjuft and haughty
" family? My heart is above indigence;
" it knows how to brave mifery and
" diftrefs; but reproach and injuries
" overwhelm and deftroy it."

When fhe finifhed her tale, fhe re-
clined her head upon the bofom of her
friend,

friend, and tears flowed down her cheeks
—in abundance.

What tended to fill up the meafure
of woe to that tender fenfible woman,
was a letter of my fifter's to me, which
fell into her hands.   I was abfent when
a negro brought it, and he feemed to
wait an anfwer.   My wife took the
liberty of opening it, and found the
following lines.

" MY dear brother, my friend,
" why would you place fo lit-
" tle confidence in her, whofe greateft
" happinefs would be to contribute to
" yours?   The perfon whom I ho-
" nour, whom I fhall ever refpect,
                              " fhould

" fhould not have known the unwor-
" thy treatment fhe has received, or
" I now deprived the pleafure of feeing
" her. Yefterday Mr. de Servens, on
" his return from my mother, appear-
" ed much difturbed. I enquired what
" had happened. Is it a long time,
" he afked me in an imperious man-
" ner, in that tone which is fo familiar
" to him, fince you have feen your
" new friend, that woman who ap-
" peared fo marvellous to you? What!
" do you mean Mr. Marfilla's relation?
" I faid. Relation or not, he warmly
" replied, is it a long time fince you
" faw her? It is fome days, I anfwer-
" ed; but I hope to pay Mrs. Marfilla
" a vifit to-morrow, when I fhall have
                              " the

" the pleasure of embracing her. It
" is very well, he said; but I com-
" mand you never to set your foot in
" that house again. Learn, he conti-
" nued in a yet more haughty manner,
" learn to know those whom chance
" presents to your acquaintance before
" you become intimate with them.
" But, I said, they are your friends,
" they are my brother's friends too. If
" your brother, he replied, knew how
" to make himself respected, and had
" been cautious of disgracing his fami-
" ly, there is good reason to believe
" we should never have seen them.
" Mr. Marsilla, I answered, is not a
" man for whose friendship you have
" occasion to blush, and his wife is of

" a very

" a very good family. It may be fo,
" he faid; but the perfon that is with
" them, is the unhappy creature that
" your brother ought never to have
" known, yet lefs to have married.
" Judge, my dear. friend, of my afto-
" nifhment, when I was informed that
" that amiable engaging woman was
" your wife. I fhall not be fo bafe, fo
" contemptible, as to blufh at being her
" fifter; her misfortunes make her ftill
" dearer to me. My friend, if heaven
" has refufed a father to her, who is
" fo worthy of your love, it has not
" granted to your fifter the hufband
" her heart would have defired. But
" I had determined never to fpeak to
" you of my diftreffes: may this let-
" ter,

" ter, my dear brother, not augment
" yours."

" *P. S.* I have yet a few words to
" say to you: but shall I be able to
" write them? Mr. de Servens went
" into your apartment, where he had
" the cruelty to order it to be stripped
" of its furniture. He bid me tell you,
" that he was not willing to offend
" my mother by receiving you. Alas!
" I read in his soul, covetous after
" riches, I see spring up again the hope
" which your arrival had destroyed.
" The most pleasing hope of mine, my
" dear brother, is to see you more hap-
" py."

Adieu.

At

At my return my wife gave me the letter, and faid to me, in a manner which indicated her diftrefs, " My deareft, " beft friend, I expofe you every day " to new troubles : you ought to hate " me."

" Hate you !" I replied, " hate her " who is the only comfort of my life! " Men may perfecute us, but they can " never ravifh my love from you ; I " will defy all the fury of fortune to " do that. But," continued I, in a fofter tone of voice, " if you forfake " me, where fhall I go ? or where find " ftrength to refift misfortunes ?"

VOL. II. E Alas !

Alas! chagrin had already affected her fenfible foul, and was increafing its ravages every day. It was in vain that her friends endeavoured to difpel her melancholy ideas, and once more bring joy in her heart; her melancholy became obvious to every one. If I reproached her gently, from a fear of lofing her; from her willingnefs to recover my drooping fpirits, fhe increafed my fears; the fmile of grief was perceptible on her lips, her tears mingled with her tendernefs, and efcaped, notwithftanding her defire to prevent them. I obferved her inclination for folitude : fhe did not avoid her friends when they came in her way, but fhe never fought them.

" You

" You are no longer happy with me,
" my tender friend," I faid to her one
day: " you feem fometimes to prefer
" being alone to feeing of me. Oh!
" you know not how neceffary you are
" to my happinefs, or what charms
" I find in liftening to you. Without
" you, could I know the fweets of
" friendfhip? It is with you that my
" friends are dear to me."

" Heaven grant that you preferve
" thofe generous friends," fhe replied;
" they will help you to fupport your
" troubles. But," fhe continued, looking at me with tendernefs, " perhaps
" you will have no more to undergo."

E 2   " What

" What is it that you fay ? Cruel
" woman !" I faid, taking hold of her
hand. " Ah! I fee that you wifh to
" die.—You wifh to leave your huf-
" band. Is it thus you ought to put
" an end to his misfortunes ? Love and
" friendfhip, have they no longer any
" power over your foul ? don't they
" incline you to wifh for life ?"

" It is overwhelmed with diftrefs,"
fhe replied. " Alas, who knows it
" more than yourfelf? Wanderers, fu-
" gitives, mifery, and contempt, have
" followed us from clime to clime.
" Falfe hope till now has fupported
" my courage: but I perceive that my
" fpirits forfake me, my faculties be-
                                " come

" come weak, my heart flutters, my
" defires, on all fides rejected, begin
" to die away. Yes, but for you, I
" could bid death a joyful welcome.
" Alas! that it would at the fame
" ftroke divide the thread of your un-
" happy days! That we could but depart
" together! — Hope, the food of the
" unfortunate, has already difappeared.
" When our friends bid adieu to this
" country, fhall we give the inhabi-
" tants a view of our indigence? Then,
" abandoned, we fhall be like thofe
" whom hunger humbles; extended
" upon the earth, they are in tortures,
" and loudly complain; the unhappy
" traveller turns afide his head, and

E 3   " goes

" goes farther off, to avoid hearing their
" lamentations."

Such were the melancholy ideas that
that tender woman, worn down with mif-
fortunes, was conftantly environed with.
Every day I faw her declining, the pale-
nefs of death was fpread over her cheeks ;
her eyes were languid, and had loft their
luftre : her face was the very picture of
diftrefs, and her fteps were weak and
flow. I was fo affected with her ftate,
that I no longer thought of either the
averfion of my mother, or uneafinefs of
my fifter. I reproached myfelf every
moment for bringing her amongft my
own family, and expofing to contempt
fo tender, fo engaging, fo good a woman :

man: her danger made me furious; hatred poffeffed my very foul; I fwore that I never would fee *her* again, who had driven me from her houfe, and fo cruelly offended me.

One day that I was with her, and uf-ing every effort to difpel her melancho-ly, we faw Mrs. Marfilla enter the a-partment.

" My dear friend," fhe faid, embrac-ing her, " behold your fifter coming to " fee you. You who are fo amiable, " fo engaging, could you imagine that " you would always be an object of " hatred and contempt?"

E 4   At

At that inftant my fifter entered the apartment, and ran with open arms to my beloved wife. She could not conceal her furprife at feeing her fo thin and changed.

She informed us, that my mother had gone the preceding evening to town; that in alighting from her carriage, fhe had met with a very bad fall, which confined her to her bed; that her hufband had immediately gone to her, and had commanded her not to leave the houfe the next day. " I am ignorant," fhe continued, " of the caufe of an or- " der, fo unjuft as to conceal from me, " from my tender embraces, a fifter " whofe

" whofe misfortunes render her ftill
" dearer to me."

Full of gratitude, my wife feemed
to take new life in the arms of her
who tenderly careffed her, who appeared fo affected with her fate, and feemed to promife her a better. Her face
became again lovely from pleafure and
hope.

Her fear, left her hufband fhould
know that fhe was come to Mrs. Marfilla's houfe, would not permit my fifter
to continue long with us. When fhe
departed, fhe told us fhe would the next
day ufe all her efforts to reconcile us
with my mother, notwithftanding the

E 5 obftacle

obſtacle which oppoſed her, and nou-
riſhed her averſion for the moſt amiable of women.

I ſent immediately to enquire how my
mother did. The next day I was informed that her danger increaſed, and
the phyſicians were doubtful of her re-
covery. I forgot my oaths, and her in-
ſults ; I flew to town. I met a negro
of my ſiſter's on the road, who told me
that I muſt come immediately, if I
wiſhed to ſee a tender mother, who was
deſirous of embracing her ſon before
death. What emotion, what diſtreſs
did I feel, when I ſaw that reſpectable
parent weak and dying, fixing her almoſt expiring looks on me, and extending

tending her hand, which I covered with kiffes, and moiftened with tears ! My prefence, my tranfports, the tender epithets by which I called her, affected her.

" My fon, my dear fon," fhe faid in a feeble voice, " I have made you very " unhappy. Where is your wife? Oh, " tell her that I pardon you your love. " If I had liftened to my heart the day " I wafted her tears, fhe would have " been near me, and I fhould have had . " no caufe to reproach myfelf."

" She has forgot all," I faid to her; " fhe regrets only the lofs of your friend- " fhip."

E 6 " That

" That I could but fee her," replied my mother, " that I could embrace her, " and call her my daughter !"

" Oh, beft of mothers," I cried, tenderly preffing her hands, " fhe will " be here, you will fee her, fhe will be " at your feet."

" It is me, yes it is me," replied my mother in anguifh and repentance, " who " ought to be at hers."

I had ordered my fifter's flave to continue his route, and tell my wife that I defired fhe would come to town with the utmoft expedition. Mr. Marfilla ordered his horfes immediately to his
chaife,

chaife, and accompanied her. Upon
their arrival they enquired for me. The
moment I perceived them, I flew to embrace them, and tears of joy and diftrefs mingled together. I led my wife
to the fide of my mother's bed.

" Behold," faid I, " the perfon whom
" you wifhed to fee."

She was willing to take her in her
arms, and call her daughter; but her
ftrength failed her, and her words died
away upon her lips. She preffed her
gently to her bofom. In ecftafy my
fifter and myfelf alternately embraced
her. In the joy of our hearts we forgot the danger of the author of our
days;

days; but the phyſicians, who then made their appearance, brought us back again to diſtreſs and fear. Their vague anſwers, their caution, made us foreſee a ſpeedy diſſolution. Her ſtrength and life evaporated in our arms. She fell into a fainting, which all the art of medicine could ſcarce recover her from. Her eyes opened to ſee her children once more, and immediately afterwards ſhe fell back in another fit. We ſaw her grow pale, tremble, and die immediately.

Mr. de Servens appeared ſoon afterwards. When he ſaw my wife and me, he could not conceal his chagrin and fears. He interrogated all the domeſticks,

ticks, and looked at his wife with fury. I was so affected, that I did not obferve his emotions. But my wife difcovered his agitations, and a maid-fervant of my mother's told her, that that man, fince he had been allied to the family, had employed his utmoft attention to in-creafe the fault I had been guilty of, in marrying without my mother's confent; that he had conftantly fpoke of the fhame and difhonour of my alliance; that he had at length carried it to that excefs, as to caufe my being difinherited by a will which my mother had revok-ed fince my return. But our laft quarrel had re-animated the hopes of Mr. de Servens; he flattered himfelf that he fhould again be able to get me exclud-

ed

ed from the inheritance of my parents ;
he had fed my mother's refentment, by
fpeaking of my diffimulation upon the
arrival of my wife, and the boldnefs
with which I had prefented her under a
falfe name.

When he was informed that fhe was
dangeroufly ill, he wifhed to fee her
without witneffes, in order to perfuade
her to give to him and his children the
valuable eftate and manfion fhe was in
poffeffion of. Overwhelmed with pain
and his importunities, my mother made
him fenfible how incapable fhe was of
executing fuch an affair at that time, and
defired him to go to her houfe in the
country;

country, and bring from thence an elixir, of which fhe had a good opinion.

As he departed, my fifter arrived. She mentioned my uneafinefs to my mother, and the defire I had of feeing her; fhe aroufed in her heart the voice of nature, and again reftored the tender fentiments which her hufband had endeavoured to extirpate. That good and fenfible mother reproached herfelf for her injuftice to her fon, and cruelty to the wife he had chofen; and her death deftroyed all the hopes of Mr. de Servens.

My wife and felf paffed in a moment from extreme mifery to the greateft opulence.

opulence. Heaven is my witnefs, that interest did not dry up the fource of my tears; in the midst of my riches I felt no bafe unnatural joy. Alas! what have thofe ufelefs riches done for my happinefs? Am I not at this time poorer than in my indigence? I had a tender and virtuous wife, whom I adored, and who loved me in return: I was then the richeft of men, and am now become the moft miferable. Oh horrid, frightful day, when I faw death ftrike my beloved wife, as the ferocious hawk ftrikes the fearful dove. My deareft wife, in vain my hands preffed you to my heart; in vain I attempted to re-animate you by my kiffes, to fhare with thee the breath of life; death fnatched you

you from my embraces. The cruel men who furrounded me, had no pity on my lamentations, my tears could not foften them. Oh, Marfilla, wherefore did you ftop my hand? Cruel friend, you have prolonged my evils; you, who promifed to return my love, have fported with my credulity ; your fruitlefs art perhaps increafed the length of her days, and the misfortunes of mine. Since that cruel moment, when the doleful knell ftruck my liftening ear, and called into the dreary tomb the only charm of my life, my heart finks under the weight of my agony. Thus the groaning flave with difficulty bears the chain he cannot break, and wafhes it with his tears; I feek with flow and

folemn

solemn pace a melancholy solitude; the head held down, the eye bedimned and fixed upon the earth, I dare not enjoy beauties of the heavens; my sight is wounded with its lustre; the pale torch which glimmers in the melancholy darkness around, is a star which pleases me most. Whilst all nature reposes, I alone roam afar, and return fatigued to seat myself on that stone which conceals from my eyes the brilliant flower which death has destroyed with his poisonous breath. If sleep sometimes close my wearied eyes, my soul seems to pass immediately into excessive woe. As soon as the bird extends his pinions, I lose myself in the forest he has quitted. I wish the moment which timid mortals fear

to

to approach; I fhould fmile at the appearance of death, as the wandering
infant who fees its mother, and extend
my arms to welcome him. Oh, moft
powerful Being, whofe breath infpires
all things, extinguifh the lamp of my
life; deign to take to yourfelf the unhappy creature who crawls upon the
earth, and unite him again to her who
formed his happinefs. *

* The wifhes of this tender hufband, who de-
ferved a better fate, were fulfilled; his two friends
had not the pleafure of feeing him long furvive
her, whom diftrefs, poverty, and prejudice, had
before cruelly condemned to the grave.

Mrs. Marfilla, whom heaven has preferved for
her venerable parents, ftill loves to converfe with
her hufband about the two unfortunates; he often
finds

finds her in tears for the death of her unhappy friend.

By publishing these memoirs, which friendship intrusted me with, I cannot flatter myself with preventing the fatal effects of prejudice, which stifles the purest sentiments, which substitutes for the light brilliant chain of love, the unhappy bond of interest. Unhappy victims of avarice and pride, will you always sacrifice your happiness and that of your children to chimeras?

End of the Memoirs of an American.

A SHORT

A SHORT

DESCRIPTION

OF THE

ISLAND OF St. DOMINGO.

THIS island, one of the largest of the Antilles, has borne different names. When it was discovered by Christopher Columbus, in the year 1492, the inhabitants called it *Haiti*; which, in the language of the Indians, signifies *mountainous land*.

It is of considerable extent, and interperfed with high mountains, at the

foot

foot of which there are very fine plains, fome of which are fifteen and twenty leagues in circumference. The French get immenfe riches from fuch as are in their poffeffion, in fugar, coffee, indigo, cocoa, &c.

This ifland is fituated in the north fea, at the mouth of the gulph of Mexico; it is not lefs than four hundred leagues round, and near a hundred and twenty four in length from eaft to weft: its breadth differs; in fome places it is not more than twenty eight leagues. The whole latitude of the ifland extends from about feventeen to twenty degrees: its longitude is not precifely afcertained.

France

France poffeffes about a third; what they enjoy extends from the river Maf-facre, in the eaftern part of the ifle to the river Neybe, the moft fouthward of any place in the poffeffion of the French.

Notwithftanding St. Domingo is in the torrid zone, the air is very tempe-rate, but feveral parts of it are un-healthy.

The French part of the ifland is in-finitely more rich and populous than that which belongs to Spain. That part contains only one capital city called Santo Domingo, and fome fmall towns where the people languifh in the greateft misery. That belonging to the French, every where presents the most flourishing appearances. Its commerce is very great: it every year employs in its imports and exports near four hundred merchant-ships from all parts of France, and loaded with riches which are dispersed over the whole kingdom. There is every where such an appearance of opulence as cannot fail striking strangers: there are some cities which are not much inferior to many in Europe, and many towns which might pass for small cities. The principal are the Cape, Port-au-Prince, where annually reside the governor and intendant; Leogane, Saint-Mark, Cayes-Saint-Louis, Little Goave, Fort-Dauphin, &c.

The

The city of the Cape, which is the capital, is fituated on the fea-fhore; its road is very fpacious, and is capable of containing more than four hundred fhips: its entrance is defended by a fort which is built on a mountain, from whence it can deftroy every veffel of the enemy which offers to make its approach. In this city a multitude of ftrangers, led thither by the hopes of foon acquiring a large fortune, fpread riches and induftry among the inhabitants. It becomes every day more beautiful and extenfive. The outfide of the houfes are very uniform: architecture has decorated them, and expelled that bad tafte which before prevailed, when they were lefs regular and fubftantial:

F 2 they

they now confift of no more than one ftory in general.

Robt Cowe,

The ftreets are ftraight and croffed at equal diftances. Among others, there is one ftreet in particular where the merchants principally refide, where intereft difplays every thing that can raife the attention and flatter the tafte of the American; but he has learned to be no longer a dupe to appearances. Lodgings are infinitely dearer here than either at Paris or London; all kinds of eatables are at fuch a price as terrify ignorant ftrangers who arrive there, and damp their hopes. What yet more tends to diffipate them, is the abundance of merchandize, which are often to be

bought

bought at a lower price than in the country where they were made. Sometimes the ftranger can fcarce guard himfelf during his refidence from extreme diftrefs, by the difpofal of what he thought would have made his fortune.

Port-au-Prince, next to the Cape, is the moft populous city, although it is new built. The buildings are not very regular, but the ftreets are very ftraight, and fhaded with trees which guard off the fun, and make the place airy. The governor has fixed it as his refidence *.

* The readers who attach fome importance to what preferves focial order, and affures men peace and equity, will find at the end of this work a defcription of the government, and the manner of diftributing juftice in St. Domingo.

It

It is not fo well defended from its fituation as the Cape.

I fhall not ftop here to defcribe all
the cities belonging to St. Domingo, as
it is an ifland generally known; hope
has led thither fo many Europeans, who
have returned again, that I fhould only
repeat what perhaps has been faid a
thoufand time before.

In the fuburbs, of the cities are different habitations; it is there the rich
American difplays all the pageantry of
his wealth; his large eftates are covered with thofe black men, whom nature
has condemned to reproach and labour.
Difperfed in the fields, they dig the
land

land for the planting of the canes, and deftroy the weeds which fpring up inconceivably faft.

In the evening thofe unhappy wretches retire to their huts, and forget, near their wives or miftreffes, the fatigues of the day, and the wretchednefs of their ftate.

No one can be ignorant of the great feverity ufed by their tyrants in the punifhing of the moft trifling offences. That barbarous treatment, which they undergo in the moft humiliating fituation, affects even them with fuch poignant agony, that a white man would die under fuch torture.

It

It has been for some time feared, that in consequence of the negroes increasing in number every day, they would in time make themselves masters of the island, and extirpate the white people. But, from studying the principles which actuate them, there may be discovered a base and servile soul, which renders them incapable of perpetrating great crimes, or opposing great virtues. Timid and fearful, their revenge is always obscure. Accustomed from the earliest infancy to a state of servitude, they are insensible to that indignation which would lead them to break the yoke, and restore the slave to his natural liberty. They console themselves in their misfortunes, and are not at all affected with

with the fufferings of their fellow-flaves, though they themfelves were their executioners. Intereft will break the league which unites them, becaufe they have no other than fuch as pleafure and debauchery have created. The moft violent paffion which the negro is fenfible of, is that of love: that inflames his heart, and makes him brave diftrefs, or even death.

There is no univerfal ftandard for the difpofitions of all negroes. The different countries from whence they derive their origin, the variety of objects which prefent themfelves, the kind of life, more or lefs laborious, to which they are accuftomed in their youth,

their

their conſtitution being more or leſs robuſt, all theſe form different ſhades in each individual, and change their native diſpoſitions in ſome degree. Amongſt ſome, a ſtupid inſenſibility makes them callous to their misfortunes and ſeverity of their maſters, whilſt a mortal melancholy attacks others, which is incurable. Several accelerate their death by ſuſpending themſelves on a tree, others by poiſon, whilſt the cruelties they ſuffer from their maſters generally inſpire them with the deſign. There are ſome, who are more cruel in their revenge, and poiſon a great number of their comrades, to ruin him whoſe property they are.

The

The American or Creole is natural-ly haughty: it is from their pride that their beſt qualities take their ſource; he is generous, and exerciſes hoſpitality in the moſt noble manner. In every ha-bitation, the traveller meets with what is neceſſary to recruit his ſtrength. He uſed formerly to be received with more confidence; but it has been ſo often abuſed, that there are no longer thoſe things ſet out, which might tempt and even diſgrace poverty.

The Creole women are tall for the moſt part, but their ſkin is not ſo white as that of the Europeans; they are in general very well formed, their ſenſa-tions are acute, and violent paſſions are

F 6 every

every where difcovered in them; they are haughty and imperious, and are born with an independent difpofition. Perhaps they might be improved, if their education was lefs neglected. The tendernefs of their mothers allow them fuch liberties in their infancy, as muft inevitably furprife a ftranger, who has been ufed to fee fweetnefs and modefty in young perfons of their fex.

The fpeculative man, who travels over the ifland of St. Domingo, would meet with fome few objects to pique his curiofity. Some wild plants which grow upon the high mountains, whofe properties are unknown to the oldeft inhabitants, might, perhaps, if fubmitted

ted to a chemical analyfis, become exceedingly valuable.

The woods have no rare animals,
nor are there any apes to be feen;
parroquets fometimes appear in great
numbers. The humming bird, whofe
plumage is very gloffy, is the moft
beautiful bird belonging to the ifland;
but it is fo very fmall and wild, and
its flight fo quick, that it is very difficult to furprife it.

Among the various productions which
make the riches of this ifland, fuch as
cocoa, coffee, indigo, &c. the principal,
and what brings the greateft advantage
to the inhabitants, is the fugar-cane.
Through-

Throughout America there is no place where it is better cultivated, grows in greater abundance, or produces more good fugar, than in St. Domingo. It grows with a top, like the dry reed: its leaves, roots and ftalk are like it, and it differs only from the common reed, by the latter being hollow, that it commonly grows taller, lefs thick, in proportion to the diftance of the knots being greater, and that it commonly grows in watery and marfhy places. The fugar-cane, on the contrary, thrives beft in the earth that is deep, and but little expofed to water, although it grows in all foils indifferently well: its rind is not fo hard as the reeds, and it is much heavier, by reafon of the pithy fub-

ftance

ftance it contains, which affords us that mild fweet juice, that by the force of fire is brought to fugar.

They may plant the canes in all feafons, provided that fome light rains precede and follow the planting, that they may imbibe earth enough to refift for fome days the burning rays of the fun, and take root.

In like manner they may cut them at any time, if 'the cane is come to maturity: but it muft however be obferved, that they will yield lefs at the time of the rainy feafons, becaufe it will occafion a very great degree of vegetation, which indeed will occafion a larger

quantity

quantity of juice, but it will be crude and vapid, and produce but little fu-gar.

The plantation that succeeds the best, is what is called a *plantation from slips*. They begin with cutting pieces of cane from fifteen to eighteen inches in length sloping from the head. When they have properly prepared the earth, they mark rows at equal distances, which ought to be two feet and a half, and sometimes four feet asunder, according to the quality of the land; they dig holes eighteen or twenty inches long, twelve or fourteen wide, and six deep, in which they place three or four plants set against each other, but a little out

of

of the ftraight line. After having placed thefe plants gently declining, upon
a little foft, light earth, they cover
them, half filling the trench, or fometimes entirely, according as the feafon
is more or lefs rainy. Thefe plants
foon pufh out ftems with tufts, and
fhoot into the earth a quantity of hairy
roots, which extend to a great depth.

The firft emoluments arifing from a
piece of cane is fixed at fifteen or eighteen months; this is what is called roll-
ing the great canes. This firft cutting
is what produces the moft fugar in the
lands long cultivated.

When

When canes are planted in a favourable foil, they will yield four or five cuttings, from the fame pieces, before replanting; but if it is dry, if it is not replanted after the firft or fecond cutting, their fhoots will then be dry, hard, and abortive, and will not anfwer the expences.

The canes which grow in light, deep foils afford fugar eafy to make, and generally fine, if they are cut at the true point of maturity. The reafon is obvious; the land contains lefs active falts; vegetation is flower; the canes produced are lefs loaded with crude phlegm, they do not grow fo high, and increafe more gently, which occafion the juice to

be

be better difpofed for the formation of fugar; and as in general they become lefs confufed, the heat of the fun penetrates them more, and they come to a more perfect maturity.

On the contrary, thofe that are planted in new, very frefh or damp foil, have fo quick a vegetation, that they become very tall in a fhort time, very thick, and extremely loaded with tufts. The fun then not being able to penetrate them, they do not arrive at the fufficient degree of maturity for the perfection of fugar.

The earlieft authors who have fpoke of the fugar-cane, have made it originate

nate in the Eaft Indies, brought from thence by the Spaniards and Portuguefe to Madeira, and the Canary iflands, and from thence to the Antilles of America. This is the generally received opinion; but Father Labat is of opinion, with fome other writers, that it never was carried to America, but that it is as natural a production of that country as the Eaft Indies. He refts his opinion upon Thomas Gage, an Englifhman, who faid, that at Guadelupe, in the year 1625, the favages brought him fugar-canes; upon Ximenes, a Frenchman, who fays, in his treatife on the plants of Mexico, that the cane grows in the neighbourhood of the river Plata; upon John Lery, who, in 1556, fays, that

that he faw it at Brazil; and upon Father Hennepin, a Francifcan, who alfo fays, that he has feen it on the banks of the Miffiffipi *, and John de Laet, at the ifland of St. Vincent. He adds, that the French have found it at St. Chriftopher's, Martinico, and Guadelupe. But what will thefe teftimonies weigh with thofe of the firft hiftorians of America, with that of the author of the Natural Hiftory of Cocoa and Su-

* Father Hennepin has certainly miftaken the fimple reed for the fugar-cane, in the lands near the mouth of the Miffiffipi. On going up that river, there are whole forefts of dry reeds to be feen, in the marfhy lands, whilft the ftagnating water is no way proper for the nourifhment of the fugar-cane.

gar,

gar, with what Rauwolff and Benſon have ſaid, atteſting that the ſugar-cane was originally from the Oriental climes. If the ſugar-canes are natives of the continent of America and the Weſt Indies too, why was there no appearance of that plant in the iſland of St. Domingo, either in the French or Spaniſh part of the iſland? There is indeed a ſpecies of the reed, but it is deſtitute of the quality of the ſugar-cane. The climate and ſoil however are as proper as the lands about the river Plata, or the iſland of Guadelupe.

There remains but little more for me to execute the deſign I propoſed, than juſt to ſay a few words about the ori-

gin

gin of the French poſſeſſions in the iſland
of St. Domingo.

The Spaniards had already extended
their empire on the continent of America : with ſword in hand they had
ſpread over that unfortunate country,
which incloſes ſuch riches in its boſom ; a
numerous race of people had made their
diſappearance, and the conquerors, all-
covered with blood, peaceably enjoyed
the fruit of their victories : veſſels loaded with gold of the new world, were
ſailing inceſſantly to inrich Spain, and
increaſe yet more their haughtineſs and
power. France and England could not
ſee without envy ſuch vaſt poſſeſſions invaded and pillaged by a people more
happy

happy than formidable: both attempted to turn the courfe of that fource, which every where diffufed fuch abundance. If thofe two nations, always divided, always jealous, had united their forces, they might have taken from Spain all her conquefts, and left them in contempt, and afhamed of their barbarities.

In 1625, the French, under the command of two captains of fhips, and the Englifh, commanded by a man named Warner, arrived at St. Chriftophers at nearly the fame time. United by intereft and neceffity, thofe two people marched in concert againft the Caribbees, who were the inhabitants of that

that ifle, and divided between them the fpoils of their enemies.

The king of Spain was uneafy when he heard that the French and Englifh had invaded the ifland of St. Chrifto-pher, and formed an eftablifhment there. He gave orders to Frederick de Toledo, who commanded a fleet fent againft the Dutch, to expel thofe new inhabitants, whofe ambition he feared. A man named Du Roffey, one of the chiefs of the French, who ought to have oppofed the landing of their enemies, having more than nine hundred men with him, fhamefully abandoned all his pofts. The victori-ous Spaniard infifted upon all the Eng-lifh and French quitting the ifle, and

VOL. II.　　　G　　　threatened

threatened to deftroy every man of them he fhould find at his return. After making them embark, he purfued his courfe.

However, the Englifh, beaten about by tempefts, and having nothing more to fear from the diftant enemy, returned again to the ifland, and were foon followed by feveral French. The reft, who had departed with their captain, being joined by feveral French and Englifh adventurers, approached the Spanifh ifland, to which has fince been given the name of St. Domingo; and finding the north fide abandoned by the Caftilians, they fettled there.

It

It coft thofe Frenchmen more trouble to maintain and increafe their poffeffions in that ifle, than the Spaniards had known in conquering the greateft part of America. They found good and fearful men who offered them refrefhments, who ferved them for guides, and who brought them the metal they were fo avaricious of. Their very princes deigned to vifit them, fent away their fuite when they approached them, and fhewed them the greateft confidence. One of them, after loading their chief with prefents, obtained permiffion to build a city in his kingdom, who gave him as much land as he would take.

If

If the thirst after gold which fired them had been extinct; if jealousy and hatred had not divided them; if a brutal haughtiness had not made their hearts callous to humanity, to gratitude, to pity, they would have been masters of the finest and most fertile countries of America; they would have found immense riches in the bowels of the earth; they would not have been debased and dishonoured by the murder of their benefactors; they would not have reduced to servitude, or punished with a shameful death, those chiefs who were too noble and generous to suffer slavery; the indefatigable Columbus would not have had his triumphant hands loaded with chains; he

would

would not have been infulted by the people whom he had enriched, and his fucceffors had never known death by poifoned arrows.

The French, on the contrary, without fupport, without fuccours, had to engage an enemy elated with fuccefs, who covered the ocean with their veffels, who waged war with them like robbers, difowned by their own country. Never-thelefs, they furmounted all the obfta-cles which oppofed their advancement, and fhortly became a terror to their enemies. The buccaneers and free-booters were the ramparts which pre-ferved that little republic, and prevent-ed the eruptions of the Spaniards. We.

G 3

will.

will give a flight fketch of thofe two claffes of men, whofe valour has made them fo celebrated.

It was very difficult for the new inhabitants of St. Domingo to attend to the cultivation of their lands. Inceffantly harraffed by an enemy who ravaged their fields, who carried away the fruits of their labour, they chofe a kind of life which nature feemed to favour, and at the fame time increafed their bravery.

A prodigious quantity of wild oxen filled the woods of the iflands: the Dutch offered to the inhabitants to purchafe their fkins, and furnifh them in exchange

exchange with every thing they might have occasion for. A number of them immediately associated together, and formed a body; united by interest, they forgot their origin, and changed their names. Unwilling to follow any longer the rules of custom, they no longer acknowledged any master; there reigned the greatest equality among them; they were willing to depend upon nature and their articles; they pulled off their clothes they used to wear, and clad themselves in a shirt dyed in the blood of animals, a pair of drawers, a large belt armed with sharp knives, a fusil, and a hanger, a hat with no brim, except before, and shoes made of the skin of wild hogs. As soon as day-light ap-

G 4   peared,

peared, thefe formidable hunters difperfed themfelves, and went a great way
into the woods, followed by a pack of
dogs. Neither the precipices, nor rug-
ged and thorny paths, could ftop them;
they broke down every thing that oppofed itfelf to their hafty fteps, their ar-
dour for the chafe raifed them above
every thing. When the beaft they purfued became wearied, the dogs furrounded it, and made the woods ring
with their barking; the buccaneer,
armed with his fufil, ran up and fired
at the beaft, who was ftruggling againft
death. More ferocious than the beaft
itfelf, he threw himfelf upon it, and
finifhed with his knife what he had
begun with his fufil, fkinned it, took
a bone

a bone from it, broke it, and, warm with the chafe, fucked the marrow it contained.

After killing a certain number of cattle, all the hunters affembled to dinner. Let any one imagine a troop of men, covered with blood, as we may fay, fpread on a plain, feated upon the ground, and devouring the meat, before the colour was well changed by the fire; all of them full of the notion of liberty, fpeaking in a tumultuous manner of their chace and their enemies, and breathing only carnage, and they will even then have only an imperfect idea of thofe favage men, who feemed to go farther from humanity every day.

G 5   This

This independent life, devoid of fear and defire, appeared fo feducing, that feveral youths of fome family, whom a fpirit of liberty had led amongft them, would not forfake them afterwards, and difdained going to France to poffefs inheritances that would inrich them.

The Spaniards ufed every effort to extirpate the buccaneers; they killed feveral of them who had ftrayed too far from their comrades; but the reft immediately reunited, and marched againft the Spaniards, who could not refift the impetuofity of their courage, and had no other means of deftroying them, than by deftroying the wild oxen. Thofe animals became fo fcarce afterwards,

wards, that the buccaneers, finding no more, were forced to live by cultivating the land, and dealing in tobacco, which, before the eftablifhment of companies, brought large fums of money into the new colony.

A great number of buccaneers, who could not comply with the uniform and peaceable life of cultivation, became freebooters. At firft, the body of the freebooters were chiefly compofed of miferable failors: embarked in their fmall canoes, which could not contain more than five and twenty men, they went and furprifed the fifhermens barks, and took from them every thing they could find. The reunion of many of the buccaneers having

G 6   increafed

increafed their numbers, they attempted greater things; they had often the rafh-nefs to go and attack large veffels, which might have eafily funk them, if chance, great expertnefs, and an aftonifhing intrepidity, had not raifed them, if I may be allowed the expref-fion, above all danger. When they were once aboard, however numerous the crew might be, they foon made them-felves mafters of the veffel; they often-times began by finking their own veffel to the bottom. Expofed to the injuries of the weather, they paffed days and nights upon the fea, in the midft of ftorms, driven about by winds, and preffed with hunger. If they perceiv-ed a veffel, it was of but fmall confe-

quence

quence to what nation it belonged; they made to it with all the fury of defpair, braved death, and ftruck with aftonifhment their ghaftly enemies. They were confidered as fo terrible, and their boldnefs had caufed them fuch amazing fuccefs, that the Spaniards dared no longer contend with them, and often delivered themfelves up, only afking their lives; but a confiderable prize only could difarm them. If they found nothing, they were implacable, and hurled into the fea the unfortunate wretches who had nothing to give them. The hiftorians relate from the valour of the free-booters things that are incredible. Antiquity prefents us with nothing equal to the heroifm and favagenefs of thefe robbers,

robbers. In the midſt of their crimes they ſtill preſerved ſome ſigns of religion. Their prayers and vows, when delivered from danger, would lead one to ſuſpect that they believed in a juſt God. But if in their courſe they went aſhore, they would ranſack the churches, carry away the ſacred veſſels and bells, and often ſpill the blood of men.

The government of Saint Domingo had occaſion for all their addreſs to reſtrain that ſavage banditti, accuſtomed to live by rapine. When any expedition was ſuppoſed to be deſigned, the inhabitants were obliged to ſtay upon the iſland to defend it, under pain of puniſhment. Mr. Dangeron, to whom

the

the French colony this day owes its flourishing condition, who facrificed, for its prefervation and improvement, his fortune, repofe, and life, found out the method of making himfelf feared and beloved by the free-booters. His courage furprifed them, and his goodnefs feemed to foften their favage difpofition. He commanded one part of them to clear the lands, and increafe the number of the inhabitants. The fate of one of the boldeft chiefs they ever had, alfo difcouraged feveral from following a life where the advantages could never compenfate for the trouble and danger. That intrepid free-booter ftiled, himfelf the Olonois; he was thus called, becaufe he fprung originally.

from

from the blacks of Olonne. He was at firſt a buccaneer's valet. His courage ſoon elevated him above ſervitude; and a deſire of diſtinguiſhing himſelf, led him to join the free-booters. He gave ſuch ſignal proofs of his valour, that he was ſoon appointed to the command of a veſſel.

It was then his talents diſcovered themſelves; his intrepidity increaſed. Although his veſſel was ſmall, he took ſuch conſiderable prizes, that he was ſtiled the Spaniards Scourge. As ſubtle as brave, he eſcaped from his enemies, into whoſe hands his raſhneſs precipitated him. In ſupporting a very bloody engagement againſt a whole army,

army, he faw all his people perifh with their arms in their hands. All his friends already dead, he trembled at the danger which furrounded him; he threw himfelf amongft the dead, by which means he became covered with blood; his enemies, not doubting his fharing the fate of his comrades, gave themfelves up to joy, and lighted fires to celebrate their victory, and his death: the Olonois arofe in the dead of the night, cloathed himfelf in the habit of a Spaniard who lay dead on the field of battle, and went to a town, where he promifed liberty to fome flaves, if they would join him in their mafter's canoe which was on the coaft; he perfuaded them,

them, and returned to the island of Tortuga.

The Spaniards soon followed them.
The governor of the Havannah, being
much irritated, sent against him a frigate mounted with ten pieces of canon,
and manned with fourscore seamen. The
Olonois had fifty men, and two canoes.
He saw the frigate enter a small river;
he advanced with his men, equally divided in the two canoes, in the night,
one on each side of the river; he dif-
embarked his men, and made a breaft-
work with his canoe, which he hawled
up behind some trees, and ordered the
same manœuvre on the other side of the
river. As soon as day appeared, all
the

the free-booters began to fire on the·
frigate. The Spaniards, who could not
fee their enemies, fired at random, and
killed none of them. The blood which
run in ftreams out of the fcupper holes
of the frigate, indicated to the Olonois
the diforder of the crew: he ordered
his canoes to be immediately launched,
embarked, boarded the frigate, and
made himfelf mafter of it. In his fury he dealt death to all who fell in his
way. A flave, trembling with dread,
threw himfelf at his feet, and promifed
to tell the truth, if he would fpare his
life. The Olonois, being furprifed,
pledged himfelf to reftore even his liberty.

"Sir,"

" Sir," said the unhappy wretch,
" the governor of the Havannah, not
" doubting our making you prisoners,
" had given orders for all of you to be
" immediately hanged, and I was sent
" to be your executioner."

When the Olonois heard this, he
foamed with rage, and ordered the slave
to bring all the prisoners to him, one
after another. The barbarian, with
his eye sparkling with rage, raised his
formidable arm against the pale trembling Spaniard, and cleft him in two,
whilst, more blood-thirsty than a cannibal, he licked the blood yet reeking hot
upon his hanger.

Guided

Guided by the flave, he went and took four barks appointed to give him chace, and pardoned only one man of them, whom he charged with a letter to the governor of the Havannah, in which he told him what he had done, and informed him at the fame time, that he would treat all the Spaniards he could furprife in the fame manner, and even himfelf too, if he fell into his hands.

The Olonois going aboard the frigate again, united himfelf with another adventurer, and then formed greater defigns. He failed to Maracaibo, in order to befiege it, though it was fortified, and very well defended from its fituation;

tion; he took that city, feized all its riches, and returned to Tortuga to diffipate the fruits of his conqueft, with his companions, who fhortly afterwards entered upon new dangers.

I will not follow that intrepid warrior in all his expeditions; I fhall only fay, that after having given a thoufand proofs of his valour and favagenefs of heart, he was one day furprifed by fome Indians, who difperfed his frighted troop, feized him, and carried him into a wood, where they roafted and eat him.

Several bands of free-booters continued to moleft the Spaniards: encouraged

raged by their fuccefs, they were no longer afraid of the numbers of their enemies. Two hundred of them took a town defended by a thoufand foldiers. The Spaniards made new efforts to ftop the progrefs of the French; they came to the Cape to attack them, to the number of three thoufand fighting men. The mif-underftanding which prevailed at that time between the governor and the king's lieutenant was more favourable to them than the fuperiority of their numbers. They landed without oppofition, and advanced into the meadow of Limonade, fo called; where, notwithftanding the courage of Mr. de Caffi, who made an obftinate defence, and died covered with wounds, they

gained

gained a battle, which restored them the ascendency they had so long lost. They had also, in the end, greater advantages; but the king, in 1696, sent a fleet from France, commanded by Mr. de Pointis, who came to St. Domingo, to augment his forces. Mr. Ducasse, who was at that time governor, furnished him with twelve hundred men, and placed himself at their head, under his orders. The fleet departed from the Cape, and sailed straight for Carthagena to besiege it. After a brave defence, it capitulated. The commander extracted immense riches from it, and basely cheated the inhabitants of St. Domingo of their share, although they most contributed to the success of

the

the enterprize, and had been always expofed to danger.

The free-booters, finding themfelves
fo egregioufly deceived, returned from
Carthagena, notwithftanding the governor endeavoured to retain them. They
laid the inhabitants under contribution
a fecond time, who gave all they had
left, to preferve themfelves from their
fury; but on their return, they were
interrupted by a fleet of the enemy,
who funk fome of their veffels, and
took from them all they had brought
away.

The injuftice of Mr. de Pointis to
them, and the very great feverity they

H
had

had been treated with, occafioned a confiderable number of the free-booters to go to Jamaica, where the Englifh had not better troops to oppofe them. It is certain that the new colony owed to their valour the fuccefs and repofe they enjoyed. Whilft they were harraffing the Spaniards, the inhabitants peaceably cleared the uncultivated lands, enriched themfelves, and put them in a condition to oppofe with equal forces thofe of their enemies.

At this time the Spaniards have no more to fear; dull indolence has. fucceeded that fury which animated them againft the new inhabitants of St. Domingo; their towns prefent a fcene of indigence

indigence and depopulation. St. Domingo is ornamented like an old palace, which befpeaks its ancient fplendor: commerce, which infpires induftry, and diffufes plenty, is loft, through the greateft indifference for riches; their numerous flocks furnifh thofe languid people with all they covet; for their fobriety greatly diminifhes their wants. The men, extended in their hammocks, are rocked to fleep by their flaves, hunger only can drag them from their beds, where they pafs the greateft part of the day; they tread with difdain the ground which inclofes in its bowels the gold that formerly they were fo covetous of. Loft in the greateft ignorance, a ftupid pride, which makes them look

H 2   upon

upon the French with contempt, a fu-
perftituous religion, which their fhameful paffions difhonour, are the only fentiments that feem ftrongly to affect
them. The connections the Spaniards
have had with the Africans, and original inhabitants of the ifle, have given to their defcendants a tinge more
or lefs black, which feems to have nearly deftroyed every trace of their firft
origin.

N O T E S.

OF THE GOVERNOR.

The governor of St. Domingo is the
fupreme of the colony. His authority
extends over all the other commanders,

ers, the officers employed under his government, and all traders. He ought
to maintain good and found difcipline
among the military, and preferve the
duty and fidelity which the inhabitants
owe to the king. It belongs to him to
give to the officers and inhabitants the
permiffion of leaving, or going out of
the colony, after the ufual publick no-
tice has been given for the fafety of their
creditors.

The governor formerly prefided over
the ifland of Tortuga, as well as St.
Domingo. At this time they have only
the title of governor general of the
ifland of St. Domingo. Their commif-

H 3   fion

fion bears date for three years, but they are often continued in the office much longer by order of the king.

OF THE INTENDANT.

The intendants were firft eftablifhed in the year 1707. The governor, before that time, ufed to do the duties now belonging to that office. Every thing that concerns government, the diftribution of the taxes raifed in the king's name, are regulated by the intendant of the colony. He alone can give orders for the fupport of the places where juftice is given, hofpitals and other buildings appointed for the publick fervice. It is to him the inhabitants

tants carry their complaints, and he ought to make the governor do them juftice.

Of the Jurisdiction of St. Domingo.

It is not fufficient to extend power, to difcover a country, and conquer it; it is neceffary to reftrain the inhabitants, the cultivators, and make them love the yoke put on them. The more alienated thofe people are, the milder ought the power to be ufed which hangs over them. There is no chain that more ftrongly binds the fubject to the monarch, and the citizen to the government, than juftice; but it is neceffary that that juftice fhould be

H 4   placed

placed upon a firm bafis, that it fhould be open and acceffible to all, that its weight fhould terrify the wicked; that neither intrigue, quirks or money, fhould be able to make the fcale preponderate.

This truth was never more obvious than at prefent; it has delivered the colonies from an arbitrary power; the governor, inftead of reprefenting a haughty tyrant furrounded by his flaves, at this time prefents the image of the prince who has depofited his power in his hands, who has placed in him the moft facred depofit, viz. the hearts of his fubjects. Poffeffions are now no longer precarious; the hufbandman, who repofes

pofes under the fhadow of the laws, no longer flies from perfecution; he is no more afraid of feeing his inheritance laid wafte, his acquifitions fnatched from him by power. The military government no longer exhibits to the honeft inhabitant a fcene of defpotifm.

There are two degrees of jurifdiction in the colony; the admiralty, and the two councils, where the appeals from the latter are judged by the former, as the laft refource, as well in civil as criminal caufes. * One of thefe councils is at the Cape, the other at Port-au-Prince. They were formerly

* The king, by an edict of March the eighteenth, created a third tribunal.

com-

compofed of a certain number of citizens, elected from the moft rich, fenfible and honeft of them, who left their habitations voluntarily, to render juftice gratis to the people; their fittings were fomerly for a month. The king, willing to give a form more permanent to his councils, and a more ready road to juftice, by his edict of January, 1766, has ordered, that the titular counfellors, the general proctors and their deputies, fhould refide at the Cape, and Port-au-Prince, and that their fittings fhould not be interrupted. His majefty appointed to each counfellor a falary of 12000 livres. By another edict of the fame year, he affigned nobility to

the

the office of titular counfellors and general proctors after twenty years duty.

Thefe employments cannot be entered upon before the age of twenty-feven. To be a counfellor, it is neceffary to attend the-bar of the parliament of Paris, or in the royal courts of juftice, for the fpace of four years.

The fovereign council of Port-au-Prince, and the fuperior council of the Cape, hold audiences three days in a week. At the firft audience, fummary caufes, and fuch as require difpatch, are pleaded in the fame manner as in the parliament of Paris. In thefe two councils, the governor holds the firft

H 6   place;

place; he has only one voice, as well as the intendant, who can assemble them upon extraordinary occasions, after giving his reasons to the governor. In his absence, his sub-delegate general presides as first counsellor. *

The legislative power is not so extensive in St. Domingo, as in France; beneficial and feodal matters are not known, nor intails and feoffments of trust; nor all those great affairs of succession and wills; their jurisprudence is not clogged with that difference of cus-

* The oldest officer in rank has a right, when the governor is not present, to assist at the council of Port-au-Prince; and he occupies the first place, after the vacant one of the governor's.

tom,

tom, which makes ours fo complex. The knowledge of the common law in matters of obligation, the cuſtom of Paris, and its decrees, are ſufficient for the counſellor who defends a cauſe, and the judge who pronounces ſentence.

I do not propoſe to examine whether the legiſlature is well adapted to the manners of the inhabitants, to the nature of their fortune, to the unuſualneſs of their caſes, the immenſe gains of the murmuring creditors, and the unhappy events which ought ſometimes to prolong the terms of engagements. A diſcuſſion of ſuch a nature would lead me too far. Man arrives at perfection by ſlow degrees; it is not till

after

after long and continued error, that he ftumbles on the road which leads to peace and equity.

I fhall not fay more of the abufe which arifes from intereft or negligence of the regifters and fubaltern officers, than that it is neceffary to reftrain their greedinefs. There are two fprings which affect all our actions; honour, and intereft. The art of government is to increafe the force of one, and diminifh that of the other.

THE INSTITUTION OF THE MILITIA.

The inhabitants of St. Domingo, till lately, were never fubject to any military fervice: the king quarters troops

in

in the colony which ought to defend it; but S. M. has created a new militia within thefe two years, the companies of which confift of the inhabitants, The governor appoints the officers from amongft the richeft and moft diftinguifhed. This inftitution laboured under fome difficulties at firft: but the feditious have been frighted, and have at length funk under the weight of authority. The duty of the militia is but light, they are only obliged to prefent themfelves in their uniforms and under arms at two reviews made every year by the governor.

This militia is nothing equal to that we fee in France, formed by the unhappy py inhabitants of the country, who reluctantly carry the arms which force has placed in their hands. It is a troop of men richly cloathed, whose appearance is very brilliant. It is divided into infantry and cavalry; the officers enjoy military honours, and are in hopes of the crofs of St. Louis.

Besides those companies, there are others also formed of free negroes and mulattoes; they are commanded by white men, and are chiefly employed in discovering the run-away slaves and deserters.

The counsellors of the superior council, the practising advocates, the members of the society of agriculture, &c.

&c. are exempt from ferving in the militia; but they are obliged to have two mufkets, and a certain quantity of powder and ball. Notwithftanding thefe precautions, the ifland of St. Domingo is fo extenfive, and fo indifferently defended by nature, that it would be very difficult to prevent a furprife, or make long refiftance againft a powerful enemy, who wanted to plunder the inhabitants of their riches.

OF THE NEGROES.

It is a very humiliating fight for man, to fee that part of the human fpecies placed in the rank of domeftick animals; but, fuch is his misfortune, that having once violated the laws of nature,

the

the evil becomes neceffary to him: becaufe he has once done wrong, he is
always to do fo; but his crime is not
unpunifhed; he is unwilling to acknowledge his like in a flave, and he dif-
covers in him the ferocious creature
that feeks to fly from, or devour the
hand which torments it. If by the effect of a wife polity, which is lefs at-
tended to, becaufe it depends more on
manners than the laws, the planters
would foften the fate of thofe unhappy
wretches, and invite them to population by their gentlenefs, there would re-
fult immenfe wealth to the colony; the
inhabitants would not give their mer-
chandife in exchange for flaves, which
commanders bring from that country
which

which intereft and war depopulate every day, and their flaves would be better and more robuft, from being born upon that fpot to which fervitude had attached them.

Thofe unhappy creatures, upon their arrival at St. Domingo, are in general attacked by that frightful difeafe, which is become more fatal to the Europeans, than the treafures of the new world has been advantageous to them. The libidinous difpofition of the negroes perpetuate it, and has made it fo common, that they have no other way of preventing their children having it, than by their being nourifhed by goats milk.

They

They are so fully persuaded at St. Domingo of the necessity of servitude, and those base maxims of punishment are so cruelly adopted, that it would be futile to examine whether it is not possible to employ free hands for the cultivation of the land; and whether it is true, that a base treatment is the only method of inticing to labour the sluggish slave; it is certain that the European would with difficulty suffer that scorching heat which the negroes bear. But because the more robust African is necessary to a delicate and proud people, is it necessary to condemn him to perpetual slavery? how much worse is his condition, than that of the beast who labours in our fields? This thought alone

alone is enough to strike the soul with horror. What a wretch must that master be, who can hear the cries of a slave with unconcern, who with dry eyes can see his blood spilt, and not stop the hand that sheds it?

OF DISEASES AND THEIR CAUSES.

Almost all the white people who go to St. Domingo, not only those who come from Europe, but also those who go from the islands and continent of America, are attacked, soon after their arrival, with a malignant fever, the symptoms of which are convulsive spasms, delirium, and sometimes lethargy. The danger sometimes continues so long as to the twenty fifth day.

To

To obviate this difeafe, it is faid to be neceffary to bleed before embarking for the ifland, and to live regularly during the voyage. The light air, which univerfally prevails at fea, occafions a great appetite: if it is too much indulged, it increafes the quantity of juices, and retards the circulation of the blood. The warm latitudes increafing perfpiration, there remain only in the veffels the groffer fluids which occafion too much refiftance to the moving fibres and propelling power of the heart: by which that equilibrium which is the principle of life is deftroyed; hence difeafes and death.

Upon

Upon his arrival, the new-comer ought to obferve the ftricteft regimen, and not fuffer himfelf to be drawn too eafily into thofe pleafures which the lafcivious African entices him to.

Another caufe of feveral difeafes to which the inhabitants of St. Domingo are expofed, is the variation of the air; the evenings, nights, and mornings, are very cold, compared to other hours of the day when the heat is exceffively great. Neverthelefs the men continue the fame cloaths, which are very light; they take no care to prevent the ill effects of the chilly dampnefs of the evening; hence arife thofe difeafes which are common to the autumn in Europe.

Of

OF PLANTS.

Beneficent nature covers the earth with her gifts; mother of all that breathe, she offers to her children her riches and bosom; she causes the tops of trees for the winged inhabitants of the air to perch on the branches, and seek for shelter against the winds; she meliorates and causes to fall the fruit which, whilst suspended, her children perhaps cannot reach; she rolls her limpid streams through the wavy fields, where the weary hunter may allay his thirst; she causes herbs to grow for the nourishment of cattle, and enamels the gay meadows with flowers, from whence the industrious bee extracts his sweets;

from

from whence likewife may be culled the falutary felf-healing plants, fo excellent in the cure of wounds. The lands of America, more cherifhed than thofe of Europe by the burning ftar that affords us day, are always in vegetation. A light fhower makes a thoufand different plants fpring up in a day, which the negroes as foon deftroy. Chance has difcovered the excellence of fome, which are carefully preferved. The tree that bears the caffia, the fena ufed by the phyficians, and the calibafh whofe fruit is very falutary; jalap, ipecacuanha, pine apples, citrons, and an infinite number of other plants, both ufeful and agreeable, afford the inhabitants of St. Domingo articles of commerce, which very much enrich thofe who cultivate them. Father Labat and Mr. Chevalier have defcribed them more fully and treated on their utility.

DESCRIPTION OF THE EARTHQUAKE.

Thefe tranfient thoughts on the government and actual fituation of St. Domingo, were reduced to writing, when the moft frighful accident diffufed diftrefs and terror, and made the inhabitants afraid of being crufhed in pieces, and buried under ruins.

The third of June, 1770, the day of Pentecoft, about a quarter after feven in the evening, there was felt an earthquake throughout the whole ifland of of St. Domingo, preceded by a dull rumbling noife like the lowing of a cow, and a confiderable commotion in a line from eaft to weft. A thick horizon, a burning atmofphere, and heavy air during the day, foretold that event. Fortunately, almoft all the inhabitants of the city of Port-au-Prince, had walked out of their houfes or into their galleries : hence they had time to throw themfelves at the firft fhock into the middle of the ftreets, which are very fpacious and fhaded with trees as we before obferved, when fpeaking of that city. The two firft fhocks, which followed each other almoft inftantaneoufly together, continued not much lefs than four minutes. During that fpace the

wind

wind was in all points of the compaſs;
it might be faid, that at that time the
earth boiled, and that it was become
fluid, for its motion imitated the waves
of the ſea. Thé moment which ſuc-
ceeded this melancholy cataſtrophe was
horrible indeed: the duſt with which
the air was filled, which almoſt prevented breathing; the groans, the lamenta-
ble cries, the heart-rending groans of
the wounded and dying; the fear of
being either drowned or ſwallowed up;
every thing in ſhort inſpired horror.
The pale glimmering of the moon, by
exhibiting the rubbiſh and ruins, ſtill
more increaſed the general conſternation
in that dreadful moment; death every
where preſented itſelf under the moſt
ghaſtly

ghaftly appearances. As foon as the people were recovered from the firft impreffion of fear, each demanded and anxioufly fought for his friends and relations : the mother who was happy enough to fee her fon again, felt in the midft of the publick calamity, joy mixed with grief.

After thofe terrible fhocks, there fucceeded feveral more, which though flighter than the former, were fufficient to deftroy whole cities: during the reft of the night the earth was always in motion and floating as it were; the different fhocks which agitated it, fucceeded at very fhort intervals, and at almoft always different fpaces of time. The

I 3   day

day at length appeared to enlighten the accident, and prefent to us the moft dreadful fight. The earth was opened in a thoufand places; the foldiers, worthy of a more honourable death, lay buried under the ruins of the barracks and hofpitals; the mountains that commanded the town were wafted and confiderably funk; the publick buildings, fuch as the governor's houfe, the intendant's, the affembly houfe, and the moft fubftantial folid buildings, fuch as the new church, the new guard-houfe, the powder magazine and fome fingle houfes, were nothing but a heap of duft; fuch was the firft appearance of the calamity experienced at Port-au-Prince. Although the number killed

at

at Port-au-Prince by this accident did not exceed two hundred, yet there is no doubt but that earthquake was more fevere than that felt at Lifbon. If we confider the breadth of the ftreets, which placed the inhabitants in fafety; if we attend to the day and hour as well as expectation of fuch an accident, which occafioned moft to be out of doors, it will readily appear that to thofe happy circumftances we owe the prefervation of our lives.

What ftill more proves that the fhocks at Port-au-Prince were more violent than thofe at Lifbon, is, that according to the moft authentic account of the misfortune at the latter place,

I 4   two

two thirds of that city refifted the violence of the fhock, and moft certainly that capital could not have refifted thofe fhocks which deftroyed and threw into ruins in an inftant the moft folid and ftrongeft buildings at Port-au-Prince.

It is neverthelefs certain that the action of that concealed force in the bowels of the earth, does not difcover itfelf every where with the fame ftrength, and that the larger a city is, the more buildings ought to efcape the commotion, which becomes weaker by extending itfelf.

The fhocks which were afterwards felt, were innumerable for fifreen days,

and

and they were even perceived for a month after the firft.

The plain, and what is called the *Cul-de-fac*, have not been more fpared than the city; all the houfes and fugar manufactories were thrown down; the earth opened and fwallowed up a great number of plantations; many houfes eftablifhed in the coffee branch were deftroyed; the river of the *Cul-de-Sac* was dry for fixteen hours, at the end of which time it returned with great impetuofity; the black mountain, another which is fuppofed to contain fire within its bowels, in a place commonly called the Whirlpool, where at all times are to be heard lowings like thofe which have

I 5 preceded

preceded all the fhocks, and the mountain of Guimbi fhattered with the commotion have deftroyed all the old
roads.

The city of Leogane experienced
the fame difafters; the church, which
was pretty and large, the meeting-houfe,
the garrifon, the powder magazine, the
military hofpital, which had withftood
the earthquake in 1751, and the terrible hurricane that fucceeded it, were
unable to refift that aftonifhing trepi-
dation, and fell to the ground; the reft
of the city was likewife in ruins, and
fifty perfons killed.

The

The plain of Leogane equally fuffered; the works, whether of fugar or coffee, were either totally deftroyed, or very much damaged; the rivers left their old, and formed new beds: the fame caufes produced the fame effects every where: it left only one houfe ftanding amidft the ruins of little Goava.

The northern part of the ifland felt lefs of it than the fouth, but it has not difcouraged the inhabitants, who are to this day employed in rebuilding their houfes: the hopes of gain, that powerful chain, has fixed them to that perilous earth, and made them forget all the dangers they have efcaped.

I 6   APPEN-

APPENDIX.

I Would have concluded the Memoirs of an American by a defcription of the manners of that people, facrificed to the fanaticifm and cruel ambition of the Spaniards. I propofed to myfelf to have difcovered the falfehood of thofe celebrated hiftorians who have loft the truth in the furmifes of a flighty imagination; who by a ftroke of the pen have raifed fuperb temples in countries where the firft rules of architecture were unknown; who have fertilized fields where depopulation and favage cuftoms have left the cultivation of the earth to

nature,

nature; who have defcribed a wife, fyftem of government, where horrid defpotifm ruled without controul ; who
have built immenfe and well fortified
cities, where none but ftraggling and
indefenfible villages were ever feen.

A philofophical writer has prevented
me.

I could have proved how much the
haughty Spaniard had impofed on our
credulity ; I could perhaps have de-
monftrated that that people plunged in
ignorance, who had no idea of naviga-
tion, who never fufpected there were
men feparated from them by immenfe

feas,

feas, were not fo numerous as they would compel us to believe.

I might have proved, that America, when the Spaniards firft entered it, was inhabited only by fmall troops of favages, who lived ftraggling, under the laws of a diftant prince, becaufe agriculture, and the fine arts, which only could form them into focieties and civilize them, were unknown. If otherwife, would the Spaniards, after fuch victories, have experienced the horrors of famine in a cultivated country? would they have found the lands every where over-grown with brambles which occafioned them no fmall trouble? Would they have been forced to kill

their

their horfes which made them fo formidable, to feed on their flefh, if great
depopulation had not caufed thofe countries to be extenfive defarts? Would
they have paffed through immenfe
forefts, without being wounded by the
arrows of their enemies, who would
have placed themfelves fecurely under
cover with their dreadful arms? In
fhort, if the Mexicans and Peruvians
had acquired that knowledge of the
arts, that the Spaniards honour them
with, there would have been feen in
their temples the veffels ufed at their
religious ceremonies ornamented with
engravings; there would have been
pictures feen, and their mythology
would have been defcribed. The fun,

which

which they adore, would have received
homage from fuch talents; there would
have been feen that bright ftar animat-
ing all nature, raifing from the bofom
of the earth the flowers which enamel
it; its image would have been repeated
a thoufand times upon the porticos of
the temples: their altars would have
been loaded with its attributes.

The chiefs of their enemies, fo zealous to carry over to the court of Spain
the grains of gold, the pearls and all
the precious trifles that the Americans
gave them, would not have failed carry-
ing in triumph the magnificent fpoils of
the temples fo much boafted of. Ma-
drid, enriched by the mafter-pieces of
opulence

opulence and tafte, would at this day have been the richeft city in the univerfe.

If fanaticifm had placed burning torches in the hands of the Spaniards, and had conducted them to the gates of the temples, where idolatry did homage to the fun; if they had put their torches to every thing that thofe worfhippers of fire employed in the adoration they paid to that planet which enlightens them, they would at leaft have fpared the cities and palaces of the Incas. But they were willing to deftroy every thing that could difcover the ignorance and weaknefs of thofe people, whom they had fo cruelly annihilated. They

They have mentioned wonders in their hiftory of the conqueft of Mexico, for the fame reafon, it may be faid, that engaged Alexander to bring fhields and bucklers of an aftonifhing richnefs.

Perhaps alfo the Spaniards, by increafing the number of their enemies, have been willing to apologize to pofterity for their unparalleled barbarity on that account, and prove to them, that it would have been impoffible to have conquered fo numerous a people, to have deprived them of their riches, if they had not ufed difpatch during their furprife to annihilate them.

A faith-

A faithful hiſtory, an exaɕt deſcription of a world ſo long unknown, and whoſe exiſtence was ſcarce ſuſpeɕted, would be a very uſeful and intereſting piɕture. What new objeɕts would have preſented themſelves in thoſe vaſt countries, where the inhabitants had manners ſo oppoſite, a form of genius ſo different ! What valuable diſcoveries might not have been made by a nice obſerver, well-grounded in the knowledge of phyſick, natural hiſtory, and phyſiology, if after having viſited with candour and juſtice the melancholy remains of that degenerated ſpecies who inhabit the new world in the centre of the torrid zone, he had afterward carried his obſervations to thoſe little, wandering,

dering, and difperfed tribes in the northern parts of America !

How many fyftems, adopted through
ignorance and prejudice, had never been
hazarded, if man had carried his obfervations further, if he had not pinned
his faith on another's fleeve ! But it is
fo eafy to broach opinions, and fo
pleafing to make them received, that
there is often more time loft in defend-
ing them, than is neceffary for the dif-
covery of truth. A philofopher cannot
but obferve and compare how much
men will fay and difpute, and irritate
each other, who have never ftudied in
their lives, nor fubjected their ideas to
experience.

Memoirs

Memoirs written by avaricious merchants or zealous miffionaries, who undoubtedly, could be but indifferently informed, have been for a long time the
fources from whence Europe has formed fuch falfe ideas of the origin and
genius of the Americans. They have
been willing to reject the truth for falf-
hood, and the whole is become one
continued error. The hands of avarice
have raked from the earth, have extracted from its bowels the gold which
it concealed; but the piercing eye of
the philofopher has not penetrated into
the heart of the melancholy and fufpi-
cious cannibal, of the Efkimaux who
feed on frozen fifh, nor of the Patago-
nian

nian who wanders fo wretchedly in folitude.

Man has braved infirmities and death
by finking into deep mines, by plung-
ing himfelf into the fea to feek for
pearls; yet is afraid to penetrate into
the midft of the frigid zone to obferve
naked and uncouth nature, which would
increafe his knowledge, and teach him
how to know the human fpecies under
every appearance.

The defire of diving into the origin
of the Americans, and difcovering the
time when the new world began to be
inhabited, is to fink into eternal darknefs in fearch of light. If the foil,

obfcured

obfcured by immenfe forefts, filled with
wild and poifonous plants, growing in
ftagnant water; if a country where are
none to be feen but weak men emacia-
ted with difeafe, the primary caufe of
which exifts in the air they breathe, and
the reptiles they feed on; in fhort, if a
dull and unfociable difpofition, which
in general prevails in monfters, whilft
the more noble and grand productions
are degenerated, pronounce an origin
not very diftant, there is reafon to fay
it was in its infancy, and that the new
world was in a weak ftate when the
European entered it.

But how many unknown caufes might
have contributed to diffufe over the furface

face of America that melancholy alteration? By how many unhappy events might the human race have again funk into that ignorance and degeneracy which characterized thofe indolent and pufilanimous beings who were drowned in feas of blood? In vain do we perplex ourfelves in conjectures on the caufes of this phœnomenon; we fhall never perhaps difcover the truth.

This is certain, that at the time America was firft difcovered, that climate was unhealthy to the human fpecies. Thirft after gold made the Spaniards furmount all dangers, and if I may be allowed fuch an expreffion, placed them out of the power of difeafe.

eafe. In the fouthward parts and moft of the iflands of America, a marfhy land, · where the waters ftagnated and became . putrid, produced · an infinite number of poifonous trees and plants: from which the favages expreffed a juice to dip their arrows in, which by only wounding the fkin gave fpeedy death.

By an unexampled fatality attached to that wretched fpecies of men, the Americans ·eftablifhed on· the eaftern fide fed upon a poifonous plant, which neceffity had infpired them with the means of making falutary. *

---

* See the firft volume of the Philofophical Re-fearches. The root here alluded to is the caffada.

Ought we then to be aftonifhed at thofe unhappy creatures, when fore preffed by hunger, devouring their ene-mies ? ought we to feek further in fuch diftreffing neceffity, the caufe of thofe horrid repafts, where man ferves as food for man ? Yes, it was only in the greatnefs of hunger and famine, that the Anthropophagi, after having fearch-ed the woods through in vain, flew up-on any other hunter that chance prefent-ed, and fixed his murdering tooth upon his limbs. When man has once vio-lated the firft law of nature, he places no bounds to his favage difpofition, and becomes more cruel than any other animal.

The

The people who cultivate peace, have gentler and more sociable inclinations : these latter formed the empires of Mexico and Peru; but these unhappy wretches had still another enemy to engage with as terrible as famine; it was a disease so dangerous and contagious, that it might be received by inspiration only, and had already carried off a greater part of the inhabitants of the new world. It is true that, by an instinct common to all animals, they at length found the means of palliating the destructive effects of that disease, less fatal in the country where it originated, than in Europe, where it has spread horrid desolation.

Such

Such was the terrible fituation of the Americans, when, to fill up the meafure of their evils, they faw a body of Spaniards land on their coafts. One of their leaders, named *Nunnez*, preceded by a pack of dogs, began by caufing one of their chiefs to be devoured by thofe animals, yet more terrible than their mafters. If we attend to the weaknefs, divifions, and ftupidity of thofe degenerate men, we cannot be furprifed at the rapidity with which the Spaniards made themfelves mafters of their empires.

The famous battle of Caxamalca, which yielded all Peru to Spain, did not coft the lives of ten foldiers. The

pioneers,

pioneers, who were the chief of the Spanish army, had under their command a hundred and sixty foot, and thirty horse; they cut to pieces and put to flight the numerous troops of Lincas Atalabila, who was himself taken prisoner, amidst his lazy soldiers, by a French pioneer.

It cost Cortez no more difficulty to conquer Mexico. The only enemies that frightened the Spaniards were the Caribbees, who, armed with poisonous darts, gave certain death, and would have destroyed that troop of barbarous usurpers, if they had made longer resistance.

What

What greatly contributed to make
the Spaniards masters of America, and
put the finishing stroke to the inhabitants destruction, was the base perfidy
of the women, who prostituted themselves to the murderers of their hufbands, who guided their steps, and
discovered to them the retreats where
the timid combatants had concealed
themselves.

Of all the people of America, those
who inhabited the northern parts of it,
or fled there, were the only ones free
from persecution, and the torments of
slavery. The Eskimaux, those misera-
ble beings, the least and most deformed of their species, from being born

in

in a country where the cold is so excessive, that trees do not vegetate, where
the ground is for nine months in the
year covered with snow and frost, continue their liberty and life.

It is in casting ones eyes over those
cold and frigid regions, that a new order of things present themselves to the
observation of the traveller; he would
imagine himself at the boundary, where
nature, weak and exhausted, had just
given existence to some rare and misera-
ble beings, whom she could not nou-
rish; yet when he considers that under
those vast bodies of ice which cover the
surface of the ocean, there swims the
Leviathan, the prodigious whale, which

grows.

grows to an enormous fize, and conftantly fwallows with its breath a thoufand animals, nature appears more
powerful, more fruitful to him, than in
thofe regions he has travelled through,
and his ideas are plunged into an abyfs
of uncertainties.

We fhall not in this appendix ftop
to defcribe the characteriftick form of
the Southern Americans, who are very
well known, as many travellers have. before treated on them. Every body knows
that they have long hair, and are of a
copper colour, which appears furprif-
ing, when we obferve under the fame
parallels of the torrid zone, black men
with woolly heads. This difference
muft

muſt be attributed to the heighth of the land, which cools the atmoſphere, which is very probable, ſince upon the high mountains, even under the line, there is a very ſharp air. The great extent of the foreſts which ſhade the earth, and continue for a long time the humidity of the ſhowers, contribute likewiſe to freſhen the air. If this is the cauſe of the different ſhade we ob-ſerve between the Peruvians and true negroes expoſed under the ſame pa-rallels, we ought not to be ſurpriſed that the people of America, more diſ-tant from the line, are as fair as the Italians and Spaniards. It would be more difficult perhaps to account for their want of beard. It has been ob-

K 5

ſerved

ferved that all the Indigenes have hair
upon no part of the body, the caufe has
been fought for in their aliments: but
there is fome reafon to think that it is
a confequence of the weaknefs of their
conftitution.

We fhall hazard fome reflections on
the manners of the Efkimaux, and
their exiftence. We are not afraid of
adopting the ideas of the author of
Philofophical Refearches, as the fyftem
appears to us, fupported upon excellent foundation. It may perhaps be
objected to him, not placing fufficient
bounds to his ideas, for having fuffered
fome contradictions to efcape him in
his work. For inftance, it is difficult

to believe him when he says, that a million of natives, at St. Domingo, were extirminated by the swords of the Spaniards, and to imagine that there are deferts on the continent of America, where population must have been greater than in the Antilles. It is fcarcely to be imagined, that men who knew the means of giving to copper the temper of steel, and forming axes and other instruments for the raifing of edifices, and cutting of stones, should have no knowledge of the arts. I doubt him equally, when he perfuades us that an European will in America, in the third generation, become as ftupid as the original inhabitants were; fince we every day obferve the defcendants of thofe

K 6 who

who firft fettled in Martinico, and St. Domingo, fhew great knowledge in their affairs. If the fciences do not flourifh in America, it is becaufe intereft fuppreffes them in embryo, and directs the active difpofitions of its inhabitants to other objects.

Notwithftanding thefe defects, the work we mention is at leaft the beft, and moft philofophical of all that have been written on America. The provoft has confulted elegance, more than truth, in his travels; he has written his memoirs in a beautiful ftyle; fuch deceitful guides lead us into error; but he has every where interfperfed fuch

beauties,

beauties, that it is pleafing to follow him even in his errors.

Dom Perneti has furnifhed fcience with fome ufeful obfervations; he has extended the knowledge of natural hiftory; but his memoirs would have been more interefting if he had had fewer of thofe trifling hiftories, and had diffufed more philofophy throughout his work.

The ftudy of the human fpecies is what feems the leaft of any to attract the attention of travellers; there are but few, who, like Mr. de la Condamine, carry among the inhabitants of diftant countries, the fearching eye of obfervation: nothing however can be more worthy their attention, than the manners,

ners, inclinations, faculties and ideas of a people when firſt preſented to their obſervation, and form ſo ſingular a con- traſt with them. We have been favour- ed with long deſcriptions of the dreſs and manner of life of the Eſkimaux, but we are ſtill unacquainted with their genius and diſpoſition. We know that thoſe little men never exceed four feet in ſtature: it has been repeated a hundred times to us, that they have a large deformed head, a flat face, a round mouth, a ſmall noſe (but not flat) full, yellowiſh eyes, unequal lips, a ſwarthy complexion, which latter ought to be attributed to the exceſſive cold they are ſubject to, the contrary extremes often producing the ſame ef- fects.

fects. We know that their short small
feet, their thick clumsy hands, indicate
their being stinted in their growth
by the cold, and never increasing to
their full size. It has been assured to
us, that those men, who appear so hideous to us, are themselves happy in
their persons, and attached to women
still more ill-favoured and deformed
than themselves are; so true is it that
beauty is only relative in our ideas.

We know that those pigmies, who
are such poltrons, so timid before other
men, encounter, notwithstanding all the
dangers of the sea, go courageously
and wage war against the sea dogs and
whales, whose oil strengthens, and for-
tifies

tifies their stomach; that their canoes
are so light and well made, that they
will always swim; notwithstanding the
waves may overset them they cannot
sink them. But it would be still more
interesting to know the ideas of those
people upon the origin of man, principle of life, and on death. If we are to
believe the author of the Philosophical
Researches, the Eskimaux have not any
ideas of a divinity, of the immortality
of the soul; their idiom is even desti-
tute of words to express it. Their industrious life, the barrenness of their
country, which obliges them to conti-
nual action, undoubtedly contributes to
that *inertia* of the mind, which has prolonged their ignorance. Perhaps they

are

are more happy, in not being tormented with thofe dull, melancholy thoughts, which inceffantly haunt thofe who deliver themfelves up to fears and dreams of futurity. The attachment they have for their country, evidently demonftrates, that man may find happinefs in the want of fuperfluities, and in a country covered with fnow and ice. The greateft liberty, and happy equality, amply compenfate for that magnificence, for that profufion, which generally accompany fervitude and flavery. They are never humbled by the prefence of a great man, nor the haughtinefs of a defpot. Huts haftily executed and built upon the fea coaft, are their palaces. Neceffity, an indiffolu-

ble

ble knot, unites them. The divifion of their fpoils, affembles them toge- ther. The Efkimaux, compelled to de- rive their nourifhment from the fea, would foon experience famine, unlefs their numbers were equally divided, one part feeking for provifion, while the other refted, and thus alternately. There is good reafon to believe that their po- verty, and the hideous appearance of their dreary waftes, will ever preferve them from the yoke of flavery. By what ftrange fatality do independance and happy fecurity, unite themfelves in that terrible climate!

If we may confide in fome travellers, they have difcovered a fpecies of men,

very

very different from that of the Eſkimaux. Giants of a prodigious ſize, of
invincible ſtrength and courage, ſpread
over immenſe waſtes, and defended from
the approach of ſtrangers: with their
robuſt and nervous arms, they raiſe up
an European as a weak timid dwarf:
the careſſes of the women, hurt the
ſtrangers who engage with them; in
ſhort, it is almoſt as dangerous to be
beloved by them as to diſpleaſe them.
The diſcovery of theſe aſtoniſhing
people have been reſerved for ſome
modern obſervers; through their per-
ſpectives they pretended to diſcover ſu-
perb temples, ruins, and immenſe gar-
dens, but on their nearer approach,
they

they faw no more than rude fketches on a wall.

What is called the defart coaft of Patagonia, is almoft deftitute of inhabitants. It is a dry fandy defart, with fome few groves of trees, but it does not produce any alimentary plants. According to all appearance the Patagonians have withdrawn themfelves into the more internal parts of the Streights of Magellan, where the foil is lefs barren, and there is greater plenty of game. The author of the Philofophical Refearches, has upon good grounds rejected the fables of commodore Byron, concerning the Patagonians, whom he had feen at Terra del Fuego.

He

He tells us in the hiſtory of his voyages, which appeared in 1765, that on
his touching at that land, his crew had
been frightened by a troop of giants,
nine feet high, mounted upon ſmall
lean horſes. After having encouraged
his companions, he courageouſly addreſ-
ſed them, and ſhewed ſuch intrepidity,
that thoſe high men, to whoſe waiſt the
talleſt of his people could ſcarce reach,
were complaiſant enough to diſmount,
and ſeat themſelves on a bank, that they
might not be higher than his crew. If
they took him and his men, as he ſays
they did, for meſſengers of heaven,
they certainly entertained no very great
idea of celeſtial beings. The women, he
continues, were ſo liberal of, and warm

in

in their careffes to him and his lieutenant, that it was with difficulty they
could difengage themfelves from their
embraces. There is good reafon to believe that commodore Byron, has di-
verted himfelf with the credulity of his
countrymen, who are extremely fond
of the marvellous. He has copied the
recitals of fome Spaniards accuftomed
to meet in the new world, with fmall,
weak, daftardly men only, and afterwards had been repulfed by favages as
tall as themfelves; who were courage-
ous, becaufe they were hunters; whofe
organization had not been nipped by
too cold an air; and whofe ftrength
had not been exhaufted by an exceffive
heat, like the people of the fouth.

The

The editor of the voyages of Dom Perneti, to the Malouin Ifles, deceives himfelf, when he fays, that the relation of a man who tells us he has feen, proves more than the opinion of a hundred who have not. How many people have feen ghofts, witches, monfters and many other extravagancies, who neverthelefs are undeferving belief? When he compares the proofs of the exiftence of thofe men, fo prodigioufly great, with thofe we may draw from nature, he will be convinced that his delight is in fables rather than truth. In fact, we ought to give more credit to Mr. Duclos, as well as to a letter from Mr. de Bougainville, who wrote to Dom Perneti in 1765: *We have made an alliance with thofe those Patagonians so much talked of, whom we have not found taller, nor yet so bad as other men.* Mr. Duclos himself does not give us any fixed idea as to the size of the Patagonians. He says that he measured some who were five feet seven inches, and that there were others much taller; but even supposing there were some who were five inches higher, they would not be of gigantick size. Mr. de la Giraudais, cited by the same author, says, that among the different acts of politeness the Patagonians shewed to his people; and what appeared most incommodious to him, was their laying themselves pell-mell, three or four upon each of his men, to preserve them from the cold. Is the European strong

enough

enough to avoid being crufhed to pieces
by fo great a weight as that of four
giants of monftrous fize extended upon,
him?

Until thofe philofophical voyagers,
after going over all the countries near
the ftreights of Magellan, fhall con-
vince us that men nine or ten feet high
exift there, and of courage equal to
their ftature, we fhall confider the Patagonians as the talleft and braveft of all
the favages that wander in any of the
known countries of America; but we
cannot believe that nature has given
them that height and enormous fize that
fome travellers have been willing to terrify our imagination with.

VOL. II.   L   What

What we have the best authenticated about the Patagonians is, that they are beardless like other Americans; that they have a large face, thick forehead, flat nose, large mouth, white and very sharp teeth, a swarthy complexion, black hair, broad chest, and large and nervous limbs. They often paint their face and body with blood. They are extremely fond of red, and received with great pleasure the pots of vermillion which were presented them. The complexion of the women is less swarthy than the mens, but they are nearly of the same stature. Travellers very much disagree as to their manner of cloathing. Some assert that they cover only their shoulders, and that when they

use

ufe any exercife they go quite naked. According to Mr. Duclos, they have cloaks made of the fkins of fea-wolves, which they throw over their fhoulders; they cover their privities with the fkin of a bird, and go with their head naked.

Mr. de la Giraudais on the other hand, gives us a long detail of their drefs; he informs us, that they are cloathed with the fkins of different animals, ftitched together like a cloak, which hangs very low; that their legs are covered with boots of the fame kind, the hair and wool of which they wear within fide; their cloaks are painted with blue and red figures, which

fome-

somewhat refemble Chinefe characters, but that they are all alike. He fays likewife, that they wear on their head a cap ornamented with feathers, like thofe of the Spaniards. Mr. Duclos and Mr. de la Giraudais, who made their obfervations of the Patagonians at the fame time, do not agree, as we have obferved, in the defcription they have given us of their drefs. The one tells us they go almoft naked, the other, covered from head to foot. If they contradict each other fo flatly upon fo evident a fact, who can believe them when they fpeak of the manners and difpofitions of thofe favages? According to Mr. Duclos they are cruel, uncouth, and thieves. They brifkly attacked

tacked his people at the moments they leaſt expected it, and are always prepared with cords to bind their priſoners with. The French were obliged to take to their arms and kill all they met with, in order too keep thoſe furious enemies at a diſtance.

Mr. de la Giraudaïs on the contrary, pretends that they are gentle, humane, and officious. One of them boldly jumped into the ſea and ſwam after a boat that was adrift; the loſs of which very much alarmed his crew. They uſed every effort to detain them amongſt them, and offered them a part of their game.

L 3   However

However frightful the life thefe people lead may be, who go a hunting
over a barren country, who have often
to ftruggle with hunger and thirft, and
are conftantly expofed to the intem-
perance of the weather, they ought to
wifh that we may never approach their
dreary waftes. There has not yet been
a voyage made to the ftreights of Magellan, that has not coft the lives of
many favages, or deprived more of
their liberty.

In the full of the moon the Patagonians make great howlings and yellings,
which would lead one to fufpect their
worfhipping that nocturnal planet: but

the

the Hottentots, who do not acknowledge a divinity, do the fame thing.

If this picture of the inhabitants of the new world is a faithful one, in what light muft pofterity view thofe barbarous conquerors, who without remorfe extirpate a people who would willingly owe their happinefs to them? Can they ever forgive them for fo cruelly abufing the ignorance and weaknefs of the Americans, whofe benefactors they ought to be? If, like their gods who taught men how to till the earth, to plant the vines and deftroy the creatures that would devour them, they had pointed out the way to the wretched inhabitants of America, the art of

improving

improving a marſhy ſoil, and purifying a corrupted air which enervated them; if they had inſpired them with horror for their abominable repaſts, their horrid ſacrifices, gratitude would have raiſed them altars, and the diſcovery of America, ſo fatal to humanity, would have diffuſed happineſs and riches over both worlds.

The ſavage, on ſight of a piece of gold, will he not ſay, it is the god of the chriſtians? For this they will quit their country, for this they come to perſecute us, to drive us from our habitations: will he not ſay with grief on the ſight of an European, If you take from us the ſmall portion of land

we

we have left, what will become of the poor Caribbee? Muſt he inhabit the ſea with the fiſh'?

THE END.

BOOKS printed for F. and J. NOBLE.

⁎ *Every Article in the following Catalogue is marked as it is fold bound, unleſs otherwiſe expreſſed.*

Adopted Daughter; or, Hiſtory of Clariſſa B—, 2 vol.   6s.
Amours of the Marq. Noailles and Mad. Tencin, 2 vol.   6s.
Apparition; or, the Female Cavalier, 3 vol.   9s.
Affected Indifference; or, the Hiſtory of Lady Conner, 2 vol. 6s.
Abbaſſai, an eaſtern Novel, 2 vol.   6s.
Akenſide on the Dyſentery, or Bloody Flux, ſewed,   2s.
Belle Grove, or the Fatal Seduction, 2 vol.   6s.
Bracelet; or, the Fortunate Diſcovery, 2 vol.   6s.
Bubbled Knights; or, the Succeſsful Contrivances, 2 vol. 6s.
Country Couſins; or, Hiſtory of Maria and Charlotte, 2 vol. 6s.
Conflict; or, the Hiſtory of Miſs Fanbrook, 3 vol.   9s.
Clementina; or, the Hiſtory of an Italian Lady,   3s.
Contract; or, the Hiſtory of Miſs Welldon, &c. 2 vol.   6s.
Captive; or, the Hiſtory of Mr. Clifford, 2 vol.   6s.
Child's Entertainer, in a Collection of Riddles,   6d
Devil upon Crutches in England,   3s.
Derrick's Letters from Bath, Tunbridge, &c. 2 vols   5s
Double Diſappointment, a Farce, by Mr. Mendez, ſtitched, 1s
Elopement; or, Perfidy Puniſhed, 3 vol.   9s.
Eliza; or, the Hiſtory of Miſs Granville, 2 vol.   6s.
Each Sex in their Humour. By a Lady of Quality, 2 vol. 6s.
Entanglement; or, the Hiſtory of Miſs Frampton, 2 vol. 6s.
Female Frailty; or, the Hiſtory of Miſs Wroughton, 2 vol. 6s.
Feelings of the Heart; or, Hiſt. of a Country Girl, 2 vol. 6s.
Force of Nature; or, the Hiſtory of Lord Sommers, 2 vol. 6s.
Farmer's Son of Kent; or, Hiſt. of Mr. Clerimont, 2 vol. 6s.
Fatal Obedience; or, the Hiſtory of Mr. Freeland, 2 vol. 6s.
Fortune Teller; or, the Footman Ennobled, 2 vol.   6s.
Female American; or, Hiſt. of Eliza Winkfield, 2 vol. 5s.
Fortunate Villager; or, Hiſt. of Sir And. Thompſon, 2 vol. 6s.
Hiſtory of Sir Harry Herald, 3 vol.   9s.
Hiſtory of a young married Lady of Diſtinction, 2 vol. 6s.
Hiſtory of Miſs Clarinda Cathcart, 2 vol.   6s.
Hiſtory of Frederick the Forſaken, 2 vol.   6s.
Hiſtory and Adventures of Frank Hammond,   3s.
Hiſtory of Miſs Sally Sable, a Foundling, 2 vol.   6s.
Hiſtory of my own Life, 2 vol.   6s.

Hiſtory